CONTENTS

3. ATHLETIC PURSUITS 53

Games that involve dashing about like a maniac.

4. ALL THE WORLD'S A STAGE 117

Games for the thespian in us all.

DRINKING AND PARTY GAMES

Geoff Tibballs

p

This is a Parragon Book
First published in 2002

Parragon
Queen Street House
4 Queen Street
Bath BAI IHE, UK

Produced by Magpie Books, an imprint of
Constable & Robinson Ltd, London

A copy of the British Library Cataloguing-in-Publication Data
is available from the British Library

Printed and bound in the EC

ACKNOWLEDGEMENTS
Illustrations courtesy of Pascal Thivillon

ISBN 0-75257-787-5

5. A BIT OF PEACE 141

Games for when you need a bit of a breather.

6. IN GOOD VOICE 177

Games of a musical nature.

7. LIFE AND SOUL 189

Meaty games for when the party is in full swing.

8. NOT IN FRONT OF THE CHILDREN 249

Games that may give cause for acute personal embarrassment the following morning.

9. DRINKING GAMES 285

Games to set you on the road to oblivion.

FORFEITS 369

Ways of ensuring that your guests remember the evening for the rest of their lives.

INTRODUCTION

All of the games in this book are adorned with amusing little symbols next to their titles. These aren't there just to make the pages look pretty, they actually have a purpose. Using the table below you can tell at a glance what kind of thing you can expect from each game. Drinking games have their own kind of symbols – see the beginning of the Drinking Games section for a full explanation.

SYMBOLS

A gently amusing game.

A very silly game that benefits from being played after a glass or two of the falling down juice.

May require you to use your brain but shouldn't result in undue mental strain.

A mentally demanding game that could result in black smoke issuing from players' ears.

A loud and boisterous game that should definitely be avoided if you have sensitive neighbours.

A game that could result in physical damage to your home or your guests – check your insurance premiums have been paid before playing.

Physical contact between players is virtually guaranteed.

Physical contact between players that is likely to result in broken homes and divorce proceedings is virtually guaranteed.

Only play this game if you don't mind being subjected to extreme personal embarrass-ment.

SYMBOLS FOR DRINKING GAMES

In Chapter 9 different symbols are used to indicate the number of drinks players can expect to consume during play. The glasses are there to give an idea of how intensive the drinking is likely to be and range from one to five plus; they do not indicate a specific number of drinks that players are likely to consume. A warning is given on page 286 that should be read before playing the games in the following chapter.

Note of Caution

Please be aware that a couple of the games involve the use of peanuts. Peanut allergies can be very dangerous, so if you are at all worried that guests may suffer from a nut allergy, it would be wise to pick an alternative game or replace the peanut with, for example, a pea.

ICEBREAKERS

You know the scene. Everybody has arrived and people are standing around inspecting their own shoes and nursing sensible drinks while attempting to engage in chit-chat. What you need is something to get your guests in the mood for an evening of uninhibited fun, what you need is an icebreaker – no, not a huge ship with reinforced bows but a game that forces people to get up-close and personal with each other.

SPOT CHECK

Object of the game

To find small objects secreted in the clothes of other guests.

What you need

A variety of small objects such as paperclips or safety pins, one different object for each player. Paper and pens for all players.

How to play

When guests first arrive, take them to a room out of sight and attach one of the objects to their clothes. The objects should be visible, but difficult to spot. Good hiding places include belts, socks, collars and cuffs. Warn guests not to mention the hidden object to anyone else and then turn them loose.

Once everybody has arrived, give each player a sheet of paper with all the hidden objects listed and a space for them to enter the name of the person that the object is hidden on. Players can be as co-operative or otherwise as they like, but they cannot deliberately make it impossible for anyone else to spot their secret object by, for example, leaning against a wall all night. The first player to spot all the objects and to correctly match them to other players wins the game.

If players know each other really well, or would like to know each other better, you could hide objects in slightly more inaccessible places such as pockets or the hems of skirts and encourage players to be a little more "hands on" with their searching.

FIRST IMPRESSIONS

Object of the game

To discover what players think of each other.

What you need

One piece of card and one marker pen per player.

How to play

This really is a pure icebreaker for a party where not many people know each other rather than a game with winners and losers. As each guest arrives, tape a piece of card to their back and give them a marker pen. As guests mingle they are required to write a short, two- or three-word description of each person they meet directly on to the card on their back.

Players should be encouraged to note down their very first impression of a person, rather than trying to form a penetrating psychological analysis. Comments such as "Nice body," or "Should lose moustache," are along the right lines.

Once a suitable period has elapsed, players may remove their cards and read them aloud. Since nobody can be sure who wrote what, the rest of the evening should be spent attempting to identify the authors of compliments.

There can be a special prize for the person with the nicest things said about them.

GET KNOTTED

Object of the game

To create the longest knotted string.

What you need

A ball of string.

How to play

Before your guests arrive cut sixty or so pieces of string of varying lengths. Most should be four or five inches long, but a few should be much longer or much shorter. Hide the pieces of string all around the house, or at least in all rooms that you don't mind guests rummaging around in. Some should be fairly obvious, others harder to find.

Divide all players into teams of two. Each team has fifteen minutes to rush around the house searching for string. Any pieces they find must be securely tied together. At the end of the allotted time the team with the longest piece of knotted string wins the game.

Another prize can be awarded to whoever finds a special coloured piece of string, hidden in an interesting location. A prize can be awarded or you can just let them keep the string.

LABYRINTH

Object of the game

A way of forming pairs for subsequent games.

What you need

Lots of string or wool.

How to play

You will need one long piece of string or wool for every two players. Before anybody arrives, wind each piece of string around every chair, doorknob, radiator and lamp in your house. One end of each string should end up in one room, the other in another room.

It's entirely up to you how far you want to go with this. You can entwine your entire house in string so that it's practically impossible to move, or you can keep the web confined to a small area. All that matters is that the ends of each piece of string end up in two separate areas.

When everybody is ready to play, send all the girls into one room and all the boys into the other (or whatever variation is most appropriate). Every player chooses a string and starts to untangle it from the furniture, winding it up as he or she goes. Players who find they are holding both ends of the same piece of string become partners for subsequent games.

AMNESIA

Object of the game

To discover who you are.

What you need

Cards that can be pinned or stuck securely to players' backs.

How to play

Before guests arrive prepare enough name cards for all of them. Name cards should have the name of a famous person on them and a safety pin. As each guest arrives, select a name card and pin it to their back without letting them see what is written on it. Once everybody has arrived and has a name tag the game can begin.

The idea of the game is for players to pretend that they are suffering from amnesia and have forgotten their own names. They may ask one another no more than three "Yes" or "No" questions about their identity before they have to move on to another player and three more questions. Depending on how many players there are you may want to let players ask the same person more then one set of three questions, but only after they have tried another player first. The first player to guess their identity is the winner, but you should keep playing until everybody has established who they are.

It's a good idea to remove or cover any mirrors in the house before playing this game (don't forget the one in the bathroom).

ABSENT MINDED

Object of the game

To spot the oddity in other guests' attire.

What you need

Paper and pens for all and guests who are willing to come to the party ready to play.

How to play

If possible, this game should be arranged a few days before the event. The idea is for players to introduce some kind of oddity into the way they are dressed that suggests they are absent minded. Examples might be a watch worn upside down, odd socks, odd shoes, or a missing earring. Players should show up dressed appropriately, but you could persuade them to do it after they arrive.

Give each player a pen and some paper. Set a time limit of about fifteen minutes for players to spot as many oddities as they can.

Make sure you have a suitably odd prize for the winner.

CIRCLE OF TRUTH

Object of the game

To lie convincingly.

What you need

A pen and paper for keeping score.

How to play

All players sit in a circle and somebody is chosen to go first — there's no advantage to this so it doesn't matter how you choose. The first player must make three statements about themselves, two of which should be true and one a complete lie. Statements should be about personal aspiration, beliefs or experiences — it's no good choosing "I have brown hair" for your lie if everyone can plainly see that you don't, but you could say "I'm not wearing any underwear" if you're willing to prove it at a later stage.

Once a player has made his three statements the other players take it in turns to guess which one was the lie. It's best to proceed with the guessing one player at a time around the circle until you get back to the player who made the statements. People should be able to remember which statement they thought was a lie, but you might want to note it down to prevent cheating. When all players have guessed, the statement maker must reveal the lie. Award one point to anyone who guessed correctly.

Continue play with the next person to the left making three statements until everybody has had a go, then total up the scores and award a prize to the winner. Depending on how many players there are you might want to play several rounds before calculating the total scores.

GHOSTS

Object of the game

To identify players disguised as ghosts.

What you need

One white sheet for every two players.

How to play

This is a variation of the classic party game Blind Man's Buff. Divide the players into two roughly equal teams by whatever method seems most appropriate – men and women is the most obvious. All the men leave the room and the women cover themselves with white sheets so as to resemble ghosts. Make sure people don't remain standing or sitting where they were when the first team left and make sure no distinguishing features are poking out from under the sheets (boots and shoes for example).

The second teams re-enters and, one by one, attempts to identify the ghosts. When asked who they are, ghosts must reply with ghostlike wails or groans. Guessers are allowed to touch a ghost's head to aid identification. If you like, the touching rule can be extended to any and all parts of the body. The winner is the player who correctly identifies the most ghosts. For the next round the women leave the room and the men become the ghosts.

PROVERBS

Object of the game

To find the other half of your proverb.

What you need

Pieces of card or paper for each guest.

How to play

Write out the first half of a proverb on each card. For example "Red sky at night . . ." Before guests arrive, write the second half of each proverb on a small piece of paper and secrete it somewhere visible but hard to spot. As guests arrive, give each one a proverb card. The object of the game is to spot the other half of your proverb before anyone else does.

Alternatively, this game can be used to form partnerships for subsequent games. Instead of hiding the second half of the proverb, give it to another guest. Players should be allowed to choose their own proverbs when they first arrive – women get to choose from the first halves, men from the second (or whatever variation seems the most appropriate). When the time comes to choose partners, the women read out their proverb halves and the men complete them.

A variation of this game is to use the first two lines of famous songs: the women sing the first line and the men sing the second line in reply.

NUMBER HUNT

Object of the game

To find hidden numbers in the correct order.

What you need

Small slips of paper, and pens and paper for all players.

How to play

Before guests arrive cut up some small squares of paper (no bigger than an inch square) and number them one to twenty. The numbered slips should then be hidden all around the house, or at least around as much of the house that you don't mind guests poking around in. They should be visible, but difficult to spot and they should be attached to a specific object. Examples of hiding places could include the hand basin in the bathroom or a picture frame in the hallway. Prepare answer sheets for each player. They should have a list of numbers and a space beside each number to enter the object it is attached to.

To make the game harder you should insist that players must enter their answers in the correct numerical order. If a player spots number three for example, he cannot write it in until he has spotted numbers one and two. If you are going to play this way you should make sure that everybody has an answer sheet with the numbers in a different order. One player could have a sheet with numbers listed one to twenty, another with them listed twenty to one and a third listed ten to twenty and then one to ten. Each player must spot numbers in the order that they appear on their sheet.

Any player can be challenged by any other player if they are suspected of cheating. As adjudicator you must check a challenged player's answer sheet to see if any answers have been entered illegally (i.e. if there are gaps in the sequence). Cheaters should be disqualified or made to wear a silly hat for the rest of the game.

FRUIT WARS

Object of the game

To topple your opponent's fruit while retaining your own.

What you need

Two spoons and two apples, lemons, oranges or similar fruits.

How to play

Two players stand in the centre of the room each holding a spoon in their left hand with their fruit balanced on the spoon. The object is to knock your opponent's fruit off his or her spoon without dropping your own fruit.

Players are allowed to move around as much as they like but physical contact, such as kicking your opponent's shins, should be strictly outlawed. The game can be played as a series of one-on-one challenges or you can organize a complete tournament with a suitably silly prize for the overall winner — two lemons for example.

KNICK-KNACK BINGO

Object of the game

To call "Bingo!" before any other player.

What you need

Large sheets of paper of card for each player (about A1 size).

How to play

Before guests arrive prepare their bingo cards by drawing a grid with nine spaces on each sheet of paper or card. The easiest way to do this is to simply draw a large, bold noughts-and-crosses pattern – two vertical lines crossed by two horizontal lines.

Once all players are assembled give them a bingo card each and instruct them to find nine ordinary things about their person. Typical objects would include banknotes, keys, earrings, rings, cigarette lighters and suchlike. Players put one object on each of the nine segments of their cards. They can put them in any order they like and people with empty pockets should be allowed to borrow from other players. You might want to have a supply of likely objects to hand. It doesn't matter if people have some of the same objects – in fact it is vital to the game that they do.

Once all bingo cards have their full compliment of nine objects, play can begin. One player is selected to go first and he holds up one of the objects on his card. Every player who has the same, or similar, object on their card can remove it. Play passes to the next player, who proceeds by holding up one object from his card. The first player to clear his bingo card of objects shouts "Bingo!" and wins the game. If the game is taking too long, the rules can be altered so that the first player to clear a line of objects from his card wins.

GUESSTIMATIONS

Object of the game

To estimate the weight of objects more accurately than other players.

What you need

A set of good kitchen scales (preferably with a digital display) and various objects of different weights. Pen and paper for all players.

How to play

An extremely simple game often seen at summer fetes, but lots of fun nevertheless. Prepare answer sheets for each player with a list of the objects and a space to enter their guesstimates. Make the objects as varied and unusual as possible to add interest, but bear in mind they must fit on the scales for the official weighing. Players should be allowed to handle the objects.

It's quite a good idea to allow lots of time for guessing. Leave the objects out all evening and then have the official weighing at the end of the party. This encourages people to attempt to cheat, which is where all the fun comes in. It's also nice to have a proper prize for the player whose guesstimations are the most accurate.

As a variation you can also include counting guesstimations in which players have to estimate the number of pages in a book or the number of strands of spaghetti in a jar. Obviously players shouldn't be allowed to examine these challenges too closely.

CINDERELLA

Object of the game

To match shoes to players.

What you need

Guests with clean feet.

How to play

As soon as guests arrive, take them to one side and persuade them to part with one of their shoes. Men should remove their right shoe, women their left. Once a shoe has been gathered from every player, assemble everyone in a circle and pile the orphaned shoes in the middle. Each player in turn picks out a shoe (not their own) and has one attempt to match it to someone in the circle. The winner is the last person to have his or her shoe identified.

Ideally this game should be played with people seated round a table so that shoes are harder to match. This puts the emphasis on matching shoes to people's personalities. In reality, even if players can see each other's shoes it's not easy to make a good match.

ALL CHANGE

Object of the game

To swap clothes with other players.

What you need

No equipment needed.

How to play

This is a pure icebreaker rather than a competition. Essentially, the idea is for guests to swap items of clothing. Exactly how you go about this is up to you. The simplest, and most modest, version involves sending all the men and the women into separate rooms and having them swap one item of clothing. Players then have the rest of the evening to identify what people are wearing that belongs to another player. Swapping underpants is not prohibited, but players would need to be on good terms to start with.

An interesting variation is to have people swap items of clothing with randomly chosen people using one of the pair-forming games listed in this section such as Proverbs or Labyrinth. Swapping between men and women is highly recommended. By far the most liberating and naughty version of this game requires players to swap their entire outfits with each other, have women swap with men and the results are about as inhibition loosening as you can get. The advantage of this game is that it gives the sensation of indulging in something tremendously risqué without actually giving cause for divorce proceedings the morning after.

MYSTERY SACK

Object of the game

To identify the contents of a sack by touch alone.

What you need

A sack or pillowcase and various objects to put in it. Pen and paper for all guests.

How to play

Another extremely simple game that can provide loads of entertainment. Before guests arrive, prepare your mystery sack. Good objects to include are things such as bottle tops, keys, small tins and corks. You will need at least ten different objects but steer well away from anything sharp or breakable. Make sure nothing is visible through the material of your sack and seal it shut with a quick line of stitching.

Players have a set time to identify as many objects in the sack as they can – about a minute is good. The only information they have to go on is what they can feel through the material of the sack. After their time has elapsed, players should write down a list of what they think is in the sack, taking care to keep it secret from other players. The player who identifies the most objects by touch is the winner.

LIAR LIAR

Object of the game

To lie convincingly.

What you need

Pen and paper for all players and a container.

How to play

Present all players with a piece of paper and a pen and ask them to write down a unique personal experience without revealing it to anyone else. Experiences should be expressed in just a few words and should be as unique and surprising as possible. Good examples include "I once met the Pope," or "I was once arrested for shop lifting." Above all, the experiences must be true. Once the player has written down their experience, have them print their name on the paper, fold it up and put it in the container.

When folded papers have been collected from all guests, play can begin. Reach into the container and withdraw one of the folded papers at random. Read the experience out loud, but do not reveal the name of the player who wrote it. All players who wish to take part in this round put their hands up, including the player whose experience it actually is. Select three players, one of whom must be the player whose name is on the paper. These three players take it in turns to fabricate the full story behind the experience, except for the author, who always gives the true facts. Everyone then votes on which player they believe is telling the truth.

This is a fun and revealing game as it is, but you can also add a scoring system. For example, players who guess correctly can be awarded points, and players who lie successfully can be awarded points based on the number of people they manage to mislead.

BRAIN REQUIRED

Exercise your brain cells and instigate a giggle-fest at the same time. Not only do these games give your guests a chance to show how clever they are, they also provide a moment or two's respite from rushing about the place with balloons and rolled up newspapers. Although some of the challenges described on these pages are suitable only for fully paid-up Mensa members, most can be tackled by anyone with a couple of brain cells to rub together.

COMPOUND INTEREST

Object of the game

To form a chain of compound words.

What you need

No special equipment required

How to play

A compound word, in the sense that the term is used in this game, is a word made up of two other short words that can otherwise be used independently. Examples would include "Houseboat," "Red-head," and "Underdog." Despite what many experts claim, there is no rational rule for distinguishing between words that are proper compounds and words that are habitually hyphenated, so you might want to take a lenient approach in the case of disputes.

The first player begins by calling out a compound word, such as "Trapdoor," and the next has to provide another compound word that uses the second half of the previous word as its first half, examples in this case could be "Doorstop" or "Doormat." Play continues in this fashion until a player is unable to come up with a follow-on word, or takes too long thinking about it, in which case they are disqualified and the next player in line starts a new chain.

A player may claim that no follow-on is possible. If no one else can think of one, then the player previous to the one who made the objection is eliminated and the challenger starts a new chain.

BOOKENDS

Object of the game

To think of words that begin and end with the same letter.

What you need

No special equipment needed.

How to play

Choose a letter at random and go around the table asking each player to provide a word that begins and ends with that letter. For instance, if the letter chosen happened to be "D," possible words might include "Defend," "Deed," "Damned," "Demand," Decried," "Dated," "Dead," and "Dud."

Take care in choosing letters. As you may have noticed "D" presents a relatively simple challenge because of the common English past tense ending "ed." Other letters, such as "J," are best avoided while "S" is far too easy if you allow plurals.

Keep going with one letter until a player declares that there are no more possible words. Deduct a point if anyone can prove otherwise, or move onto another letter if they can't.

This game requires some brainpower but gets much funnier after a few drinks.

ODD ONE OUT

Object of the game

To spot the item in the list that shouldn't be there.

What you need

Pre-prepared lists and pen and paper for all players.

How to play

This one requires quite a bit of preparation, but it's an excellent means of allowing people to show off their useless knowledge if you have friends who like to do that sort of thing.

Prepare lists of things that belong in the same categories, and then add one item to each list that doesn't belong, but could conceivable do so. Lists should have at least ten entries and can be as obscure as you want to make them. An example might be something like this: Earth is Room Enough, The Stars Like Dust, To Live Forever, The Currents of Space, The Martian Way, The Naked Sun, The Caves of Steel, The Gods Themselves (all are Issac Asimov novels, apart from "To Live Forever"). Tailor your lists to fit in with the interests of your guests. Prepare between ten and twenty lists for a game of decent length.

Number each list and give players two minutes to study them before requiring them to write down the odd one out. Unsurprisingly, the player who spots the most out of place elements wins the game.

CONNECTIONS

Object of the game

To spot the hidden link between three seemingly unrelated objects.

What you need

Pre-prepared connections.

How to play

Like many of the games in this section, you will need to put in some preparation time to make this game worth playing.

A simple example of a connected trio could be "Jeep," "Gestapo," and "Radar." The connection here is not, as it first seems, the Second World War, but the fact that all three words are acronyms (Jeep from General Purpose Vehicle, via the abbreviation GP; Gestapo from Geheime Staatspolizei; and Radar from Radio Detecting and Ranging).

In this case it would be enough for a player to point out that they are all acronyms, they needn't provide the words from which the acronyms are produced.

THE BUTCHER'S DOG

Object of the game

To recall and add to a growing list of adjectives.

What you need

No special equipment needed.

How to play

The first player thinks of an adjective beginning with the letter "A" that could be used to describe the Butcher's dog, such as "Agile," and announces "The Butcher's dog is agile." The next adds another, beginning with the letter "B," and recites "The Butcher's dog is agile and boring."

Continue in this fashion until the multi-faceted character of the Butcher's dog is fully revealed as "Agile, boring, condescending, devious, enchanting, familiar, generous, haughty, ignorant, jealous, kind, lewd, mesmerizing, naughty, opulent, prissy, quiet, relaxed, studious, terrifying, unambiguous, vile, wary, xenophobic, young and zealous." Any player unable to add a new adjective, or unable to remember the correct sequence of adjectives, is eliminated.

Once you reach "Z," start again with "A," or play a round of The Dustman's Budgie for variety.

HOSPITAL

Object of the game

To memorise an ever-growing list of diseases.

What you need

No special equipment needed.

How to play

This game gives players the unpleasant task of imagining that they are visiting a hospital that contains cases of every disease, complaint, condition and illness known to man – definitely not one for the faint-hearted.

Player one begins by describing the first disease he saw on his or her rounds of the hospital with the words "On my rounds I saw a case of anaemia." Player two must remember the first condition and add another to the list in alphabetical order. Soon players will be reporting cases of "anaemia, boils, colic, diarrhoea, embolism, foot and mouth disease, and gout."

Continue until nobody can think of another disease, or until people start feeling queasy. Medical students and hypochondriacs should be excluded.

I LIKE . . .

Object of the game

To identify the reason for a player's likes and dislikes.

What you need

Pen and paper all round.

How to play

A mentally taxing game that necessitates sitting still and thinking for protracted periods of time. Only to be attempted with guests who have attention spans longer than the average five-year-old.

Players have ten or fifteen minutes to come up with a list of seemingly irrational likes and dislikes. There is, however, a method to the madness. Consider the following list:

I like holes, but I don't like ditches.
I like handles, but I don't like knobs.
I like power, but I don't like energy.
I like slaughter, but I don't like killing.
I like dates, but I don't like figs.
I like groves, but I don't like copses.

The key to the approved-of items on this list is that they can all be preceded by the letters "Man" to create another word (manholes, manhandles, manpower, manslaughter, mandates, mangroves). The disapproved-of items do not make words when "Man" is added. Lists should include at least six like-don't-like pairs.

Players listen intently as a list is read out and the first to spot the linking factor wins the round. Alternative links could include words with a certain number of letters, words with certain vowel combinations or words that begin and end with the same letter.

SLOW CROW

Object of the game

To guess the rhyming answers to simple conundrums.

What you need

No special equipment needed.

How to play

Players take it in turns to come up with rhyming adjective-noun combinations and definition-like clues for their solution. Taking the title of the game, Slow Crow, as an example, a clue might be something like "A black bird in no hurry." "A securely stored amphibian" could be a "Stowed toad," and "A tightly constricted bosom" is clearly a "Trussed bust."

The first player to hit upon the correct solution wins a point and provides the next definition.

INITIALS

Object of the game

To answer questions using words that begin with the letters of your initials.

What you need

No special equipment needed.

How to play

Players are required to devise answers to questions using words that begin with the same letters as their initials. Questions can be provided by a well-organized host or thought up on the spot by other players. Either way, they should provide plenty of opportunity for imaginative and amusing responses. Examples might include "What meal would you most like to eat?" "What kind of people do you find most attractive?" or "What would be your ideal job?"

Bernard William Theakstone might reply to these inquiries with the information that "Bananas with tofu" is his favourite meal, that "Butlers wearing trilbies" turn him on and that he would be suited to a job as a "Ballerina who types." It's hard to see how this game could be made into a competitive sport, but some kind of recognition should go to the player that provides the most consistently amusing answers.

FIRST AND LAST

Object of the game

To compile a list of objects in specified categories.

What you need

No special equipment required.

How to play

Create a list of broad categories, such as cities of the world, famous actors, book titles or animals, and choose a player to start on the first selected category by naming one person, place or thing that fits into it. The next player then endeavours to find another member of the category that starts with the same letter that the previously mentioned item ends with.

Choosing cities of the world as a category play could proceed something like this: London, New York, Kathmandu, Ulan Bator, Riga, Aberdeen, Newcastle, Edmonton, Novgorod, Daytona and so on. Any player unable to think of a new member for the category is eliminated, as are players who repeat an entry.

Play should continue until just one player remains. Then have him or her choose the next category.

I LOVE MY LOVE

Object of the game

To describe a lover and their habits in words starting with the same initial letter.

What you need

No special equipment needed.

How to play

Another game that taxes players' word power by constraining them to use words starting with the same letter. Each player must repeat a formulaic description of their lover using the letter subsequent to the one used by the previous player. The first player, for example, informs her fellow guests that "I love my lover because he is ardent and analyzes acquisitions. I hate my lover because he is amoral and acts aggressively. My lover's name is Adam and he is from Addis Ababa. I took him to Albania and bought him some apples and apricots."

Play then passes to the next player who must describe his or her lover in the same terms but using words beginning with "B." Continue through the alphabet until undue hesitation forces you to eliminate all but one player, or until players start to adopt glazed stares.

WORD DISASSOCIATION

Object of the game

To add to a list of disassociated words.

What you need

No special equipment needed.

How to play

The polar opposite of a word-association game, this little exercise in word play relies for its entertainment value on players finding ingenious associations where none apparently exist. Participants take it in turns to come up with words that have no connection whatsoever with the word that has gone before. At any point a player may challenge on the grounds that there is indeed a connection between two sequential words, and wins a point if he or she can prove it to the satisfaction of the majority.

An example of play might go something like this: "Orange, carbon, streetlight, shoelace, Barnstable, cufflink, raisin, hat box, leek. . ." A devious player could have interceded between "shoelace" and "Barnstable" to point out that Cushing and Sons of Barnstable have been manufacturing shoelaces since the nineteenth century and are well known for it among a certain class of people who can habitually afford to have their footwear hand-made. The fact that this is completely untrue is neither here nor there, it's the smoothness with which the fabricated connection is introduced that counts.

Connection challenges can, of course, also be genuine. "Carbon" and "Streetlamp" in the above list could conceivable be associated by pointing out that some streetlamps use carbon filaments in their bulbs.

TWENTY QUESTIONS

Object of the game

To identify a mystery object.

What you need

No special equipment needed.

How to play

The original and best guessing game, Twenty Questions also has the quality of explaining its most critical rule in its title. One player begins by thinking of an object, animal, plant or person and informs the others whether what he has in mind is animal, vegetable or mineral in nature, or any combination thereof.

Other players then ask question that may only be answered "Yes" or "No" in an attempt to discover what the mystery object is before they use up their allotment of twenty questions. In case anyone was wondering, people are considered to be animals, except in the case of Long John Silver, whose wooden leg might qualify him as an animal vegetable hybrid, and Margaret Thatcher, who was notoriously metallic and therefore mineral in nature.

Guessing the correct answer wins the chance to think of another object, and keeping the other players guessing beyond the twenty-question limit wins the right to have another go and to torture people for the rest of the evening by not telling them what you were thinking of.

STEPS

Object of the game

To produce a list of words beginning with the same letter, each one longer than the last.

What you need

Pens and paper all round.

How to play

A letter is selected at random and players have ten minutes to come up with a list of words beginning with that letter. The only snag is that each word in the list must be one letter longer than the previous word. Plurals are not allowed and every step must be completed for the longest word to count – in other words it's no good writing down a ten-letter word until you've thought of a nine-letter word to precede it. The player who produces the longest step list wins the game.

Here's an example of part of a step list for the letter "S":

S
SO
SOP
SOFT
SHAFT
SINGLE
SOPHIST
SABOTAGE
SOLOPSISM
SABBATICAL
SACRAMENTAL
SCHOOLFELLOW
SADOMASOCHISM

THANK-YOU LETTER

Object of the game

To compose a thank-you letter for an unknown gift.

What you need

Pre-prepared cards, and pen and paper all round.

How to play

Players take on the role of grateful recipients of slightly suspect presents. It could be a leaving present from work colleagues, a wedding present from distant relatives or a Christmas gift from granny. Write a list of suitable gift items, such as toasters, hand-knitted jumpers, wine coolers, paperweights and naff stationery sets. Write each gift on a slip of paper and on a piece of card.

Each player draws a slip of paper and settles down to write a short thank-you letter imagining they have received the specified gift. The letter should praise the imaginary gift and its qualities and detail the ways in which it will make their lives fuller, richer and more rewarding (imagine the gift is from a very rich and ailing relative if this level of enthusiasm seems incomprehensible when applied to a vibrantly-coloured polyester necktie).

When all thank-you letters have been composed, each player stands up in turn and reads out their effort. The twist comes in the use of the cards. Before a player begins to read, select a card from the pile with the name of a present different from the one the letter has been written about and show it only to the other players. As the reader eulogizes about the generous gift of a hot water bottle in terms of its "usefulness in bed on cold nights" and its "remarkable ability to retain heat for hours on end" listeners who have seen the card bearing the word "Electric Screwdriver" should have occasion for the odd chuckle.

DEVILISH DEFINITIONS

Object of the game

To create a string of definitions for words that rhyme.

What you need

No special equipment needed.

How to play

One player volunteers to start and thinks of a word and another word that rhymes with it. Good examples would be something like "Plate" and "Hate." He or she then gives the first word and a definition for the second word to the next player, who must correctly identify the second word and come up with a definition for a third rhyming word. Play should sound something like this:

Player 1: Plate. An extreme dislike for something.
Player 2: You mean "Hate," what you do at a bus stop.
Player 3: You mean "Wait," a narrow, connecting stretch of water.
Player 4: You mean "Strait," arriving after an agreed time.
Player 5: You mean "Late," a wooden box.
Player 6: You mean "Crate," to show how something is done (demonstrate).

Any player that hesitates unduly, is unable to provide the word defined by the previous player or fails to come up with a new definition, is eliminated from the game. Challenges should be allowed against inadequate definitions or words that blatantly fail to rhyme.

A FEW GOOD LINES

Object of the game

To identify a series of books or films from a selection of lines.

What you need

A pre-prepared list of quotes and pen and paper all round.

How to play

Preparation for this game requires the host to read books at length and to delve into obscure films. If neither of these appeals to you, and would be unlikely to appeal to your guests either, this is probably not the game for you.

Select three lines from a book or film script that don't mention the names of major characters, places or identifiable themes in the work, but which could be considered representative of the author's style. Repeat until you have culled some text from at least ten or fifteen books or movies. Write the lines out in groups of three and label each group alphabetically.

Assemble all participants and arm them with a pen and piece of paper each before proceeding to read out the first group of three lines. Players have the simple task of identifying which work they think the lines come from. Once you have worked through all fifteen groups, award points according to the accuracy of players' guesses. Give one point for the correct period, two for correct period and author's name, and three for period, author's name and correct title.

GHOSTS

Object of the game

To avoid spelling-out a complete word.

What you need

A pen and paper may be useful for keeping a record of play.

How to play

Another classic pastime that, like Hangman, reinforces the odd connection between word games and the macabre. Ghosts is known worldwide under a huge variety of titles, but the rules are essentially the same whatever you happen to call it.

The idea is for one player to start spelling a word by giving the first letter of that word. The next player, not knowing what word the first player had in mind, must add another letter that contributes to the spelling of a word that he has in mind. For example, the first player begins with the letter "R," perhaps thinking of the word "Rind" (it doesn't really matter at this stage). The second player adds "A," thinking of the word "Rare." The next player may add "I," thinking of the word "Rain." What he or she must not do, however, is to add the letters "T" or "P" since these would form the finished words "Rat" and "Rap" respectively.

As the list of words grows longer, and it becomes increasingly difficult to add letters without spelling a completed word, other players may challenge an added letter on the suspicion that it has simply been plucked out of the air rather than selected with a genuine word in mind. If a player is unable to prove that the choice was deliberate by producing the word he or she had in mind, they are eliminated. If, however, they can produce a valid word, it is the challenger who is shown the door.

An elimination allows the next player in line to start a new chain of letters. Continue in this fashion until only one player remains.

For incorrigible brainiacs, try playing the game backwards. Start with the last letter and add letters prior to it until a word is unavoidably spelled out.

MOVIE BUFFS

Object of the game

To answer trivia questions.

What you need

A movie reference book.

How to play

A quick and easy way to stage a trivia quiz without all the hassle of preparing questions. Simply take a movie reference book, open at any page and read out the title of a film. Players are awarded points for each piece of relevant information they are able to provide. Points categories could apply to director's name, year of release, star's name, names of supporting cast members and basic plot details.

Clearly, this version of the game is only going to provide entertainment for serious movie buffs, but the same idea can be applied to practically any reference book from popular music to steam locomotives of the Great Western. Make sure you keep a stock of good reference books on your shelf so you can choose the most appropriate on the night.

QUOTATIONS

Object of the game

To come up with quotations containing common words.

What you need

No special equipment needed but a dictionary of quotations would come in handy.

How to play

A game for the truly erudite since it requires an encyclopaedic knowledge of famous quotations and the ability to produce apposite examples at the drop of a hat.

One player begins by citing a quote relevant to the events of the evening. Since this is a party setting "When women go wrong, men go right after them," some of the immortal words of Mae West, might be considered appropriate. Any guest who is able may chip in at this point with another quote that includes a word (or perhaps just an idea) from the first. W. C. Fields' "A woman drove me to drink and I never even had the courtesy to thank her" would fulfil both criteria admirably.

If your guests need a little help, provide a printed list of quotations at the start from which they can choose from.

FACTS AND FALLACIES

Object of the game

To spot the deliberate mistakes in a short essay.

What you need

Pre-prepared essays.

How to play

A game for inveterate swots, know-it-alls and show-offs that allows players to display their useless knowledge in a safe and controlled environment.

Prepare a short (two hundred to two hundred and fifty word) essay on a subject of historical or scientific interest. Suitable topics might include The Life of Abraham Lincoln, The Greenhouse Effect, or The Films of Marilyn Monroe. Crucially, however, your text must include a number of factual errors. An easy shortcut is to take an article from an encyclopaedia or other reference book and re-write it introducing plausible errors.

When everyone is sitting quietly at their desks, read the essay out loud to them. At any point a player may call out "That's wrong!" if he or she thinks something sounds fishy. Correct challenges earn a point, or two points if the player can provide the correct version. Incorrect challenges lose a point.

The key to preparing a good essay is to leave the big, well-known facts alone and to tinker with the minutia instead. In the case of "The Life of Abraham Lincoln" for example, everybody will remember where Lincoln was shot and the name of his assassin, but they are unlikely to be as sure about where he actually died, or what state John Wilkes Booth originally came from.

PERFECT PAIRS

Object of the game

To guess the paired identities of other player couples.

What you need

No special equipment needed.

How to play

This game requires pairs of players to adopt secret paired-names or terms, such as Gin and Tonic, Rock and Roll, Bill and Ben or Tom and Jerry, so you might want to prepare a list of suitable pairings beforehand. Alternatively, couples can think up their own names.

One pair is elected to go first and the rest of the players ask them questions along the lines of "Are you animals?" or "Are you famous people?" to try and discover their secret identities. Questions can, of course, only be answered "Yes" or "No." The first couple to guess correctly becomes the next to be subjected to questioning.

Continue playing until all identities have been revealed. Prizes could be awarded to the most original of perplexing pairings. Something like The Power and the Glory or Burke and Hare (the grave robbers) could keep players guessing for hours.

FORBIDDEN WORDS

Object of the game

To avoid using the forbidden word.

What you need

Pen and paper.

How to play

In this taboo-game one player starts by secretly writing a common word on a piece of paper. This word, unknown to the other players, becomes the forbidden word. By asking subtle questions the first player attempts to get the others to say the forbidden word, while they try and work out what the word is from his or her line of questioning.

In a round where the forbidden word happens to be "Bank", for example, the questions might go something like this:

"Where do you keep your money?"
"What do you call the land immediately beside a river?"
"How does an aircraft turn in the air?"

It should quickly be obvious to the other players what the forbidden word is, but avoiding it is another matter. Players must provide intelligible and reasonable answers without undue hesitation. Failure to do so, or committing the cardinal crime of actually using the forbidden word, results in instant elimination. Questioners who use their own forbidden words should be subject to performing a particularly horrendous forfeit.

TRAVELLERS

Object of the game

To compile a sentence with a verb, adjective and noun all beginning with the same letter.

What you need

No special equipment needed.

How to play

Seat all players in a circle – or an octagon, or an oblate spheroid, depending on taste – and choose someone to start. This lucky participant gets to turn to his or her neighbour and inquire "Where are you going for your holiday?" to which the neighbour must reply citing a country beginning with the letter "A." If you like, a city or region of the world could be given instead.

Not satisfied with this information the starting player next asks "And what will you do when you get there?" The reply must contain a verb, an adjective and a noun all beginning with the letter "A," so a valid answer might be something like "Award avaricious academicians."

Having completed his or her task successfully, the "A" player turns to the next in line and asks the same questions, this time expecting answers beginning with the letter "B". Continue around the table and through the alphabet in this manner until the player lumbered with the letter "Q" shrieks and exits the room at speed.

ACRONYMS

Object of the game

To pretend that real words are acronyms.

What you need

No special equipment needed.

How to play

An acronym is a word formed from the initial letters of a descriptive set of other words. Well-known pure acronyms include "Scuba" (Self-Contained Underwater Breathing Apparatus) ,"Wysiwyg" (What You See Is What You Get) and "Wasp" (White Anglo-Saxon Protestant). Slightly impure acronyms are often used by organisations to shorten otherwise unwieldy titles – examples include "CAMRA" (CAMpaign for Real Ale), "ASH" (Action on Smoking and Health) and "OPEC" (Organisation of Oil Exporting Countries). The object of this game is to perform the acronym-forming process in reverse – to take an existing word and imagine what it could stand for.

To begin you will need a list of five or six words. These can be selected beforehand or simply elicited from the assembled players. Words shouldn't be too long (four to six letters) and should be as evocative as possible. Good examples would perhaps include "Brat," "Skunk," "Dead" and "Strip."

Players working in pairs have ten or fifteen minutes to come up with the full names of organisations that might legitimately use these acronyms. For example, BRAT could stand for the Boring

Reactionary Atheist Tendency or DEAD for the little-known Drains Earthworks And Ducts society.

ALLITERATIONS

Object of the game

To recall an ever-growing list of alliterations.

What you need

No special equipment needed.

How to play

Another memory-taxing game that has the added twist of requiring players to devise alliterative phrases on the spot. The first player begins by thinking of a two-word alliteration that fits with the word "One," such as "One winsome weasel." The next player in the circle must recite the first player's alliteration and come up with a three-word example to add to it. For example "Two terrifically torpid terrapins and one winsome weasel." Player three could continue the trend with "Three thoroughly thoughtless thuggish thistles, two terrifically torpid terrapins and one winsome weasel."

Continue in this fashion until some poor beggar trips up around "Seven seriously seditious superannuated self-serving silver-sided sea lions," and start again while they attempt to deal with a dislocated tongue.

CATEGORICAL

Object of the game

To provide items beginning with the same letter that fit into a set of categories.

What you need

A set of categories and pens and paper all round.

How to play

Prepare a list of six or seven fairly broad categories such as Famous writers, Animals, Countries, Foods, Rivers, Cities and Film titles. Select a letter of the alphabet at random and allow players five minutes to write down an item for each category beginning with that letter.

A complete list for the letter "S" for example might look like this:

Sitwell (Edith), Stoat, Somalia, Strawberries, Seine, Seven.

Compare players' lists at the end of each round and award one point for every correct entry and two points for every entry that doesn't appear on any other player's list. Play as many rounds as seems compatible with players' boredom thresholds using a different letter each time.

A slightly more challenging version of this game takes the letters of a randomly selected keyword to provide the initials for category items. Taking the same category list as above and using

"Scare" as the keyword players would need to produce a table something like this:

S   C   A   R   E

Writers: Shelley (Percy), Clancy (Tom), Austin (Jane), Rowling (J.K.), Eliot (George)
Animals: Springbok, Camel, Aardvark, Racoon, Elk
Countries: Sweden, Cambodia, Andorra, Romania, Ecuador
Foods: Shrimp, Coriander, Apple, Radish, Eel
Rivers: Stour, Congo, Amazon, Rhine, Euphrates
Cities: Sao Paulo, Cincinnati, Ankara, Rangoon, Edinburgh
Films: Shining (The), Carrie, Ants, Rocky, Elephant Man (The)

SMALL BEGINNINGS

Object of the game

To guess words with the same prefixes from simple clues.

What you need

Prepared word lists and pens and paper all round.

How to play

Prepare a list of words with the same prefix and clues to go with them. Common prefixes include "Mis," "Pre," "Dis," "Imp," "Con," "Pan" and "Sub," so a relevant word list could be "Disharmony," "Dissonance," "Dishearten," "Displaced" and "Disagreement."

Players attempt to identify members of the word list from clues such as "A 'Dis' that's out of tune," (Disharmony) or "A 'Dis' that isn't where it should be," (Displaced) or "A 'Dis' that can't concur" (Disagreement). Work through fifteen or twenty clues and then check how many words players have managed to decipher. For the game to work properly only words with proper prefixes can be used. "Dishcloth" for example begins with "D, I, S" but isn't a valid word, whereas "Disinherit" is perfectly acceptable.

TRANSFORMERS

Object of the game

To transform words into other words by altering just one letter.

What you need

Pens and paper all round.

How to play

A four-, five- or six-letter word is selected and all players write it at the top of their sheets of paper. The aim is to create a cascade of words down the page by changing just one letter in each case. For example, if the original word happened to be "Foot," a chain could begin with the change to "Fort" and continue with "Sort," "Port," "Pork," "Pock," "Sock," "Sack," "Pack," Pace" etcetera.

Clearly, the longer the original word, the more difficult the challenge. If nobody can think of a first transformation within a few minutes you should think about switching to an easier word, or a game that involves more agitation and less cogitation.

ATHLETIC PURSUITS

You can't beat a good romping game, although a good romping game can certainly beat you if you've not been keeping up with your trips to the gym. Practically every game in this section has the potential to cause damage to your home or, even more amusing, your guests. So lock up the cat, put your knick knacks out of harm's way and prepare to get your guests rampaging about the place like a bunch of over-excited five-year-olds.

CITRUS RELAY

Object of the game

For team members to complete a relay race with an orange held in an unusual way.

What you need

A few oranges or lemons and a clear space.

How to play

Divide players into two equal teams and then pair-up team members, preferably into couples of similar height. The first pair from each team steps up to the starting line and places the orange so that they are holding it between their foreheads.

On the word "Go!" both couples must make their way across the room to a string or line placed about five yards away and then return to the start. The orange must stay in place the whole time and neither player can touch it with their hands.

If an orange is dropped the pair must replace it (using hands) before continuing. When a pair arrives back at the start the orange is then passed to the next pair who must complete the same task. The first team in which all couples finish the course wins the game.

FOX AND DUCKLINGS

Object of the game

For the mother duck to protect her fledglings from a marauding fox.

What you need

Plenty of space.

How to play

This game is a fun variation of tag that really needs to be played outdoors or in a large hall — the dance floor at a wedding reception would be an ideal venue. Choose one player to be the fox, preferably someone reasonably fit and fleet-footed. If you like, you can require him to wear a pair of fox ears or a big shaggy wig to emphasise his beastly qualities.

All players, except for the fox, form up in a line behind the mother duck putting their arms around each other's waists to create a chain of ducklings. It's the fox's job to pick off the ducklings one at a time from the back of the line. The mother duck has to prevent this happening by tearing around with her chain of ducklings in tow — she can also be armed with a rolled up newspaper if you wish. The fox is not allowed to physically push the mother duck out of the way so, as long as she remains facing him with her ducklings trailing behind, they will be out of reach. When a duckling is tagged he or she drops out of the game.

With several players it should be quite easy for the fox to pick off the first few victims, but as the chain becomes shorter it will take a lot more legwork and sideways feints to reach the remaining ducklings. There is no real winner to this game, except for the fox who gets a free workout.

BALLOON BOUNDING

Object of the game

To race with a balloon held between your knees.

What you need

An inflated balloon for each player (plus a few spares) and lots of space.

How to play

Just one of the multitude of silly things you can do with balloons, this game is best played outdoors or in a large space. Set up a clear starting line and finishing line before play begins to avoid petulant arguments between guests.

Every player gets an inflated balloon and holds it between their knees. Round balloons are traditionally used but you could use long ones to good comic effect. With their balloons clasped securely between their knees competitors must hop to the finish line. Anyone who drops their balloon has to retrieve it before continuing, or has to go back to the start if you're feeling really mean. A burst balloon means disqualification.

If this game seems a bit too energetic it can also be played as a waddling race. Players still hold the balloon between the knees but must employ a kind of waddling walk down the full length of the course.

BREATHLESS PING PONG

Object of the game

To propel a ping pong ball using the power of your lungs.

What you need

Several ping pong balls and a large table.

How to play

Divide players into small teams – about four or five to a team. Two teams position themselves at opposite ends of the table and a ping pong ball is placed in the centre. The object of the game is to get the ball off the end of the table belonging to the opposing team – but players must hold their hands behind their back and propel the ball by blowing it.

Getting the ball off the opposite end of the table scores one point and the game should be played to twenty-one points (or less if everybody smokes heavily). When points are scored, or if the ball goes off the side of the table, the referee should replace it in the middle before play continues. For a more refined game you should equip players with drinking straws to blow through.

PUFF DADDY

Object of the game

To propel a ping pong ball over an assault course using the power of your lungs.

What you need

A ping pong ball, several objects to act as obstacles and a large, flat playing area.

How to play

Before guests arrive set up the course. Think in terms of a crazy golf course for inspiration. Use books or other hefty objects to create barriers and dog-legs that the ping pong ball must be propelled around. If you're feeling particularly creative you could try building bridges, tunnels and ramps to add interest.

Players take it in turns to blow the ping pong ball along the length of the course as quickly and accurately as possible. The player who gets his or her ball from one end to the other in the shortest time is the "Puff Daddy".

You might want to equip competitors with drinking straws to blow through but this isn't necessary.

ANKLE BITERS

Object of the game

To race other competitors while handicapped in a bizarre pose.

What you need

Lots of space and something to mark a starting line and a finishing line.

How to play

The game is essentially a simple, if very silly, race between two points. Set up a starting line and a finishing line before play and equip them with stop-action cameras if you have particularly competitive friends.

Players form up on the starting line and race to the finish line. The only drawback is that they have to race while holding tightly on to their own ankles. Any competitor who lets go of his or her ankles at any time, or who falls, must return to the starting line.

Men with overly tight trousers or women with short skirts might want to consider sitting this one out – by far the most entertaining aspect of this game is watching other people make complete fools of themselves anyway.

JOURNALIST

Object of the game

To assemble segments of fragmented headlines.

What you need

A stack of old newspapers and some pieces of card.

How to play

This game combines a treasure hunt with some need for thought on the part of players. Before guests arrive, cut a dozen or so headlines from your newspapers. Each headline should be seven or eight words long and preferably in different typefaces or cases. Once you have selected your headlines, cut them into fragments one or two words long. Short words should be left with more significant words so the headline "DRIVER SHOCKED AS SHEEP EMERGES FROM POTHOLE" could be divided up into "DRIVER / SHOCKED AS / SHEEP / EMERGES / FROM POTHOLE."

Glue each fragment to a card and find hiding places for them around the house. On each card that has the first word of a headline you should write "Headline One," or "two," or "three," or whichever it is and note the number of words in the headline so searchers know how many cards they are looking for. Cards should be hidden in visible, but not obvious places.

Once guests are assembled, give them half an hour to find as many cards as they can and attempt to form them into the correct headlines. This game could be played in two teams with team members allowed to barter cards with each other. Additional prizes should be given for wrong but amusing or apposite headlines composed from available cards.

BROOM HOCKEY

Object of the game

To propel a rag into the opposing team's goal using a broom.

What you need

Two brooms, four chairs, a rag and a large smooth floor area.

How to play

Anyone who has watched ice hockey will know what a rough and tumble game it can be, so this one should be restricted to players of a young and fit disposition with adequate medical insurance.

Divide players into two equal teams (or boys against girls if you prefer) and have them stand shoulder to shoulder at opposite ends of the room. Place a chair at each end of the lines of players. These are the goals – their size determined by the number of players on a team. Number each player from left to right so that, in a five-aside game, both teams have players numbered one to five. Place the two brooms and the rag puck in the centre of the playing area and stand well back.

To start the game, the referee calls out a number – "Three!" for example – and the player numbered three on each team makes a dash for the brooms. Using a broom each player attempts to sweep the puck towards the opposing team's goal. Other team members can try to impede its progress with their feet, but this carries a very real risk of bruised ankles. At any point the referee can call out another number and the two broom-wielders must immediately down tools and make way for their team mates whose number has been called.

The game can be played to a set number of points, on a time limit, or until the less fit players can no longer hobble the length of the room.

RIGHT DOWN THE MIDDLE

Object of the game

To bisect a length of ribbon in the fastest possible time.

What you need

A reel of ribbon and two similar pairs of scissors.

How to play

Before guests arrive, prepare several sections of ribbon of equal length. They can be any length you want but bear in mind that the longer they are the more difficult the challenge. To play, give a length of ribbon to each player and a pair of scissors. Usually only two can play at a time, but if you happen to have lots of identical pairs of scissors lying around there's no reason it couldn't be more.

The challenge is simple to say but fiendishly difficult to do. Competitors must use the scissors to neatly cut along the entire length of the ribbon, splitting it into two halves. The first player to complete the bifurcation wins the game and gets to wear the ribbon in his or her hair for the rest of the evening. It's quite likely that one or both players will snip right through their ribbons in their haste to beat each other to the end, in which case the winner will have to be judged on the quality of his or her incision up to that point.

As a fun alternative, you could have cutters starting at opposite ends of the same piece of ribbon and racing to reach a point marked half way along its length. Remember that playing with scissors can be dangerous, so be careful.

EGG TOSSING

Object of the game

To toss eggs between team members without breaking them.

What you need

Two lengths of rope or string and some eggs.

How to play

A very simple game that is little more than an excuse to hurl eggs at people – an activity universally recognised as being good for the soul. Needless to say, this is best played outdoors or in the house of somebody who has a large staff of well-paid cleaners. Lay out the two ropes parallel to each other and about ten feet apart. Divide players into two equal teams and supply each team member with an egg.

Teams divide themselves so that half of their members are standing behind one line and the other half are behind the other. At the signal, players hurl their eggs to team mates behind the opposing line who must catch them using one hand only. Two-handed catches result in immediate disqualification. Continue hurling eggs back and forth until only one team has any intact eggs and is declared the winner.

To liven things up even more position opposing team members alternately behind their line and insist that throws are made over the shoulder. Barging into opposing team members to ruin their catches is strictly illegal and should be heartily encouraged.

BELL BASHER

Object of the game

To swat the elusive bell-wearing fairy.

What you need

Blindfolds, newspapers and some bells.

How to play

Another game intended to turn normally sane and peaceful people into rampaging, newspaper-wielding hooligans. The action can be enormously entertaining to watch but absolutely must be played in a space cleared of obstacles and preferably with a soft floor.

Choose one player to be the bell-wearer, this can be a highly dangerous occupation so it should perhaps be assigned as a punishment for losing, or wining, another game. Blindfold all the other players and arm them with rolled up newspapers. The job of the bell-wearer is to prance about avoiding the blows aimed at him or her by the other players. In scenes reminiscent of The Living Dead the blindfolded aggressors lurch about in pursuit of their prey, flailing wildly and causing considerably more damage to each other than the bell-wearer.

In the unlikely event of a direct hit on the bell-wearer the player who scored it becomes the next person to take on that fraught occupation.

SARDINES

Object of the game

To locate a hidden player and squeeze into their hiding place.

What you need

No equipment needed.

How to play

This favourite of children's parties can be enormous fun and provides ample opportunity for unwarranted body contact between players of the opposite sex. For anyone who led such a sheltered childhood that they have never played the game, explain the rules as follows.

One player is chosen to run off and hide. He or she should choose a cupboard or other enclosed space. After a given time, switch off all the lights in the house and set the other players loose to hunt the hider down. The twist is this; when a player locates the hider he or she must join them in their hiding place while trying to remain as quiet as possible.

As successive players find the hiding place, they too must squeeze in as best they can. In theory the last player to find the hiding place becomes the next hider, but in practice there is so much giggling and groaning as bodies pile on top of one another and bottoms are discreetly pinched that nobody can possibly tell who was last into the heap.

CHOPSTICKS

Object of the game

To collect scattered peanuts using chopsticks.

What you need

Chopsticks and a cup for every player and a bag of peanuts.

How to play

Scatter peanuts around the playing area, or simply put peanuts out in a bowl and wait for guests to scatter them of their own accord. Each player gets a pair of chopsticks and a cup and has to get down on their hands and knees and collect as many peanuts in their cups as possible in the allotted time. Obviously peanuts can only be picked up with the chopsticks, and that includes those that end up back on the floor after cups are tipped over.

Chinese or Japanese players should be handicapped by having to use the chopsticks in their left hand, or you could play the game with competitors armed with a pair of cocktail sticks instead.

BACKHANDER

Object of the game

To pass objects along a line of team mates.

What you need

Several slippery or otherwise tricky-to-handle objects.

How to play

Suitable objects for this game might include a hot potato, a wet bar of soap and a bowling ball. There should be about three times as many objects as there are players and they don't all have to be awkward to handle.

Divide players into two equal teams and have them stand in two lines facing each other. Place half of the objects next to the first player in each team line. The object is for players to pass the objects, one at a time, down their team line and then back again. The catch is that, on the return journey, objects must be passed behind players' backs rather than in front of them. This causes all sorts of problems as team members try to cope with objects being passed down the line from one direction, while others are being passed back again. The first team to get all its objects back to the starting position wins.

Bear in mind that objects are highly likely to be dropped at some point or another, so don't use your best commemorative plates. You may want to penalize teams that drop objects by insisting that the offending article must return to the beginning of the line to start its journey again.

IDENTIKIT PICTURES

Object of the game

To identify famous faces from fragments of photographs.

What you need

A stack of magazines featuring famous people and some card.

How to play

Prepare for play by selecting ten good-sized photographs of famous people's faces from the magazines and cutting them out. All the faces should be of roughly the same size and, ideally, on the same kind of paper. When you cut out the faces, make sure you remove any trace of background as well.

Once you have your faces, cut each one into four strips so you have hair, eyes, noses and mouths. Stick each of these strips on to separate pieces of card and give each card a separate number. Finally, position the cards around the house. You shouldn't actually hide them, but some should be harder to spot than others.

Give each player a pen and an answer sheet that lists the ten famous people and has four columns for them to note down the relevant card number for hair, eyes, nose, and mouth. Players have half an hour to identify as many parts of faces as they can. After everyone has had a few more drinks the cards can be usefully employed in infantile games of the Mr Potato Head variety.

THE NAME GAME

Object of the game

To memorize which name goes with which face.

What you need

Pictures of non-famous people and pen and paper for every player.

How to play

Go through magazines or local newspapers and pick out ten good-sized pictures of non-famous people. Cut them out and photocopy them so they are all black and white and the same size. You should try and choose faces that are as similar as possible so try and stick to a category such as old men or Asian faces. Assign names to each face. Use ordinary names and try to make some of them sound as similar as possible – Anne, Anna, and Annabel for example. Stick the faces on to cards and distribute them around the house in easy to spot locations.

When all guests are assembled, give them half an hour to wander around and try to memorize which name goes with which face. After the allotted time period is up, collect all the cards and put them in a safe place away from cheating eyes. Wait awhile before holding the competition to give everyone a chance to forget everything they've tried to remember.

After a suitable period, say another half an hour, assemble all the players and give each one a pen and a piece of paper. Ensuring that the names are covered up, hold each card up in turn for a few seconds. Players have to write down the name they think goes with the face. Make sure you stack the cards you have shown in the same order that you display them. The player that manages to identify the most faces is the winner.

If you want to be really sneaky you could use an entirely different set of faces for the identification round and see how long it takes your bemused guests to catch on. Alternatively, include just one rogue face and watch as competitors confidently jot down answers that can't possibly be correct.

SQUEEZE

Object of the game

To cram as many objects a possible into a matchbox.

What you need

An empty matchbox for each player.

How to play

The object of the game is extremely simple; players have a set time to cram as many different objects into their matchbox as possible. For a more leisurely and thoughtful game you should give a deadline several hours away giving more scope for ingenuity. One vital rule: all the objects must be different – fifty seven matches doesn't count, neither does twenty seven thousand grains of sand or six point two billion oxygen atoms.

Players should be allowed to roam anywhere you don't mind them going, including outside. Hosts should take care to lock up small items of jewellery if they don't want them disappearing into the pockets of absent-minded guests.

BALLOON BASH

Object of the game

To burst a balloon with a rolled up newspaper.

What you need

Several inflated balloons, a blindfold and a newspaper.

An excellent way to release pent-up stress that is yet another in the long list of silly things you can do with a balloon. Choose one player to be the first balloon basher and equip him or her with a blindfold and a rolled up newspaper. All the other guests form a circle around the basher and a balloon is tossed into the ring. Amid frantic cries of "Bash the balloon!" and "It's behind you!" the balloon basher attempts to smash the rolled up newspaper down on the balloon.

A basher has three attempts to hit the balloon, helped or hindered by the other players as they feel the need. You should probably include a rule that precludes holding the balloon down with one hand while battering it with the newspaper in the other.

Points are scored as follows: one point for a good square contact and three points for a bursting blow, making a maximum possible score of five. After the basher has delivered his or her three blows the next player goes into the ring. The winner is the player with the most points, ties being resolved by a sudden death play-off.

FAN THE FISH

Object of the game

To propel a paper fish across the floor by flapping a magazine at it.

What you need

Paper, magazines and string.

How to play

Before guests arrive cut the sheets of paper into the shape of fish. Use A4 sheets and make one fish for every player. Once the competitors are assembled, drape a length of string across one end of the room to act as a starting line, and another across the other end as a finishing line. Give each player a paper fish and a magazine.

The idea is for players to propel their fish across the floor by frantically flapping their magazine behind it, with the prize going to the first fish-flapper across the line. A referee should keep a close eye on the race to guard against illegal shoving contacts between fish and magazines.

The tendency is for most players to thrash their magazines so wildly that their fish go fluttering off in random directions. After a while people should realise that a gentler, more controlled magazine wielding technique yields much better results.

GARDEN OF EDEN

Object of the game

For Adam to catch Eve.

What you need

A blindfold.

How to play

A variation of Blind Man's Buff that is an excellent, if a little energetic, icebreaking exercise. All but two of the players stand in a large circle marking the border of the Garden of Eden. The two left over players are Adam and Eve. Whether you have a male Adam and a female Eve or vice versa or any combination thereof is entirely up to you. Either way, Adam is fitted with the blindfold and enters the circle with Eve.

Standing in the centre of the Garden, Adam calls out "Where are you, Eve?" and Eve must reply "Over here, Adam." Adam then attempts to catch her. Eve must reply whenever Adam calls her, and she must remain in the circle at all times. Set a time limit of two minutes and if Eve hasn't been caught in that time, another player takes her place and Adam stays where he is. If Adam does manage to catch Eve, she dons the blindfold and must attempt to catch a new Adam.

This game could certainly be played as a pair-forming game for other games, especially as the blindfolded player doesn't know for sure who he or she is pursuing. Other players in the circle pretending to be the pursued Adam or Eve is of course strictly against the rules and, as such, is a good thing.

ROCKET TO THE MOON

Object of the game

To propel a plastic cup along a string using breath power only.

What you need

Two lengths of string and two disposable paper or plastic cups.

How to play

Prepare two pieces of string about ten or twelve feet long. Punch a hole in the bottom of each cup and thread one length of string through each one. Ensure that the cup can slide smoothly along the string — it's probably best to use some kind of nylon twine rather than rough "hairy" string.

Divide players into teams of three. Each three-man team consists of a mission controller, a pilot and a Moon base commander. The pilot has by far the hardest job so make sure it goes to the team member with the most puff. The Moon base commander and the mission controller each hold one end of the string, keeping it taught. The pilot has the task of puffing like a mad thing to blow the cup/rocket along the string to its destination. Other team members can offer unhelpful suggestions along the lines of "Blow harder, we're losing," or "Keep going, you're almost there!" The first team to get its rocket to the end of its string wins the race.

KICK THE BUCKET

Object of the game

To evade the guards and kick the bucket.

What you need

A bucket and lots of space.

How to play

An energetic and boisterous game best played outdoors or in a roomy padded cell. Elect one sturdy individual to act as guard (two, if there are more than about eight players) and have him stand by the bucket. The bucket should be placed near a wall or fence so that access to it is restricted to just three sides.

Players attempt to dodge past the guard and land a hefty kick on the bucket. The guard's job is to prevent them doing this by tagging anyone who comes within reach. Tagged players must go and stand by the wall until somebody releases them by kicking the bucket. The game ends when everybody has been captured or when people start collapsing from exhaustion.

If you like you can include a scoring system that counts bucket kicks and subtracts tags, but it really isn't necessary.

SCAVENGER HUNT

Object of the game

To locate an example of all the items on a list.

What you need

Pre-prepared lists of scavengable items.

How to play

There are two guaranteed ways of getting people out of your house but, since one of them involves setting fire to your soft furnishing, you might want to try a scavenger hunt to get your guests out of your hair for an hour or so.

Prepare for the game by compiling a list of items to be scavenged. Take your time and give it plenty of thought – the whole enjoyment of this game depends on an imaginative and amusing scavenger list. You can be as bizarre or risqué as you like and include anything from "Half a piece of string" to "Underwear belonging to another player." In general though, objects shouldn't be too hard to locate within a short walk of your house. Take care to make the items specific – "An oak leaf" is better than "A leaf."

It's traditional for scavenger hunts to be carried out in teams of two or three – pairings could be formed using one of the pair-forming games in the first section of this book. Further enhancements might include handcuffing team members together, binding their ankles in a three-legged race manner, or simple requiring them to wear silly hats before setting out onto the streets.

BY A NOSE

Object of the game

To guide a ball across the floor using only your nose.

What you need

Two lengths of string, a tennis ball for each player and a space cleared of furniture.

How to play

Set up a racecourse with strings laid out for starting and finishing lines. Competitors line up on hands and knees along the starting line with their tennis balls placed strictly on the line.

On the word "Go!" racers but their noses to the grindstone and attempt to nuzzle their balls across the finishing line before anyone else. Players who use any part of their body other than their nose to propel their ball should be sent back to the start line.

You could award additional prizes for the most creative use of puns referring to "Balls" or "Winning by a nose," but it's not healthy to encourage that kind of thing.

TRAIL OF DEATH

Object of the game

To negotiate an extremely dangerous-looking obstacle course while blindfolded.

What you need

Various mean-looking obstacles and a blindfold.

How to play

This is more of a practical joke than a game and as such can only be played once with the same group of people. The idea is for the victim to be ushered into a room and shown an extremely daunting obstacle course involving teetering chairs, expensive breakables, carpets of upturned drawing pins and scattered marbles. The unsuspecting guest is encouraged to examine the layout of the course and to try and memorize it. After a couple of minutes he has to choose a trustworthy "guide" from among the other players who are in on the joke and is then led outside.

In the time it takes for a blindfold to be securely fitted to the victim, all of the obstacles in the room must be cleared away in absolute silence. After sufficient mucking about testing the efficacy of the blindfold, the nervous victim is led back into the room. The guide then spends several minutes leading the blind man around the non-existent obstacles accompanied by gasps from observers as he apparently narrowly avoids piercing his feet with a dozen tacks or cracking his head on a low shelf.

When it becomes impossible to suppress outright laughter any longer, the victim's blindfold is removed and the evil depths to which his friends are capable of sinking is revealed to him.

ARE YOU THERE MORIATY?

Object of the game

To wallop opponents over the head with a rolled up newspaper.

What you need

Two blindfolds and two rolled up newspapers.

This game re-enacts the last confrontation of Sherlock Holmes with Professor Moriaty, using rolled up newspapers in place of cunning and deductive reasoning. Like Fruit Wars it can be played as a series of one-on-one rounds or as a tournament.

Two players are blindfolded and given a rolled up newspaper each. Since the object of the game is to hit your opponent over the head you might want to substitute inflatable toys or foam bats for the newspapers, and Sunday editions should definitely be avoided.

Players lie face down on the floor, each one grasping their opponent's wrist with one hand and their weapon of choice with the other. One player asks "Are you there, Moriaty?" and the other must reply "Yes, I'm here," before slithering out of the way of the blow that the questioner aims towards the sound of his voice. If the newspaper scores a clean blow to the head, the striker wins the game, otherwise it's the other player's turn to ask "Are you there, Moriaty?"

PIGGY BANK

Object of the game

To put money into a piggy bank while hampered by oven gloves.

What you need

A pair of oven gloves for every player, lots of pennies and several piggy banks.

How to play

Ideally you should have one piggy bank for every player but, unless you're collector of oddities, it could be difficult to lay your hands on enough of them. If this is the case, the game will have to be played as a team game with one or two piggy banks per team.

Place trays heaped with pennies at one end of the room and the piggy banks at the other. Equip each player with oven gloves and set them ready to start near the trays of pennies. On the word "Go!" players scramble to pick up a penny, carry it across the room and deposit in their piggy bank (or their team's piggy bank). At the end of the allotted time, the player who has deposited the most pennies wins.

Dropped pennies may be retrieved or abandoned, depending on what individual players think will be easier, but at no stage may players remove their oven gloves. Also, only one penny may be carried per trip.

IN YOUR SHOES

Object of the game

To locate your shoes in the dark.

What you need

A room that can be darkened.

How to play

More of a melee than a game, this can get a little rough and invariably leads to inadvertent body contact, which can be a good thing or a bad thing depending on your luck and whether or not you get caught.

Assemble all players in one room and have them remove their shoes. Participants then retreat to the edges of the room and turn their backs while you mix the shoes up into a chaotic jumble. Next, stand well back and turn off the lights.

Players race to the shoe pile where they attempt to locate their own shoes and put them on, all in the dark. Once everybody has, what they believe to be, their shoes on, or has given up or has been trampled into the carpets like so much raspberry jam, turn the light back on and examine the results.

If you like, players wearing one or more shoe that doesn't belong to them can be required to perform a forfeit, such as tending to the wounded.

PILGRIM'S PROGRESS

Object of the game

To move forward in a distinctive manner.

What you need

A large open space.

How to play

All Pilgrims who wish to participate line up side by side. The first player in line must move forward a few feet using a distinctive manner of locomotion. Obvious examples include hopping, walking backwards, crawling and skipping.

The next player in line must move the same distance using an entirely different method. Continue up and down the line until a player is unable to think of a new method and has to drop out. The last player left in the line wins the game.

Players who drop out will probably be needed to form a committee that can rule on whether hopping on the left leg is the same as hopping on the right and other thorny issues that are likely to crop up as players strain their imaginations and limbs to find new methods of covering ground.

A special prize can be offered for the most novel way of moving forward.

FEATHER FINISH

Object of the game

To race without losing your feather.

What you need

A plate and a feather for each competitor.

How to play

A variation of that sport of kings, the egg and spoon race. Here, the objective is to keep a feather on your plate as you race other players to the finish line. Plates must be held at the edges and, obviously, there must be no physical contact with the feather.

The surreptitious use of spit, hair gel or Superglue to secure feathers to plates should be guarded against with vigilance and spot checks. As to dropped feathers, racers can be allowed to replace them before continuing, or required to return to the starting line depending on how vindictive you are feeling at the time.

SPOT THE ODD

Object of the game

To spot out-of-place objects.

What you need

Pen and paper for all players and a reputation for having a well-organized house.

How to play

Before guests arrive, wander around the house and place objects in incongruous spots. Examples might include shampoo in the kitchen, potatoes in the bathroom and slippers on a coat hook. About ten incongruities should be enough. This game only works if you aren't the kind of person who is known to habitually leave engine oil in the fridge and toothbrushes in the dishwasher.

Once players are assembled, issue them with a pen and piece of paper each and turn them loose with fifteen minutes to spot as many out-of-place objects as they can. The winner is the player who locates the most incongruities, but the real interest of the game is in discovering exactly what other people think is odd or normal. If nobody mentions the pasta in your sock drawer you have to face the dilemma of wondering if nobody found it, or of accepting that nobody thought it was unusual.

HORROR STORY

Object of the game

To scare the bejeezus out of your guests.

What you need

Pre-prepared props that can be mistaken for dismembered body parts in a darkened room.

How to play

More of a story-telling exercise than a game this should get hearts pounding and, done correctly, can elicit delightful shrieks from highly strung guests. To prepare you will need to compose a short story of gory murder, it doesn't need to rival Stephen King, just a straightforward account of an imagined murder that occurred "in this very room" and the mutilations that the victim was subject to after their demise.

The point of the exercise is that, as the story is recounted in a darkened room, props resembling the various hacked-off body parts are passed around the unsuspecting listeners. As you recall how the murderer gouged out his victim's eyes, slip a couple of peeled grapes into the hands of a guest and chuckle with glee as she shrieks and faints on the hearth rug. Severed hands can be represented by rubber gloves filled with sand, the sliced-off tongue by a piece of cold meat and the scooped-out brain by a wet sponge.

The overall effect is enhanced if the storyteller paces around the room and drops his props into the laps of guests at random. Imagine the fun to be had as a dear friend runs screaming from the room after you drop a cold, clammy hand onto their shoulder.

BROOMSTICK DERBY

Object of the game

To race other competitors while riding a broomstick and balancing a potato on your head.

What you need

Two or three brooms, plastic plates, potatoes and lots of space.

How to play

Divide players into two or three equal teams with about four or five in each. Each team gets a mount (a broom), a plastic plate and a potato. The racecourse can be as long or short as you like, but it should bring racers back to their original starting position. Racing out to a halfway marker and then back again is a good option. If you're feeling particularly adventurous, a modest jump or water hazard could be set up too.

To race, a player must stand astride his broom, place a plastic plate on his head and balance a potato on the plate. Brooms are held in place with one hand and plates with the other. Players are not allowed to touch their potatoes, except when they inevitably roll off and have to be retrieved.

Racers must remain astride their brooms all the way around the course, even when retrieving lost potatoes. On achieving the finishing line, the broom, plate and potato are passed to the next team member. The first team to get all its members around the course wins the cup, which should of course be full of Champagne.

With brooms and unsteady competitors coming into play this game really requires an outdoor setting. Appoint stewards to rule on photo finishes, illegal use of the whip or potato-handling infractions.

SOCK STRESS

Object of the game

To put on as many pairs of socks as possible.

What you need

Lots and lots of socks, gloves for every player and a room that can be darkened.

How to play

All players should be issued with gloves and told to put them on. Ideally they should be thick and unwieldy gardening gloves or, better yet, oven gloves rather than of the hand-tooled calfskin variety. All participants must be barefoot. The huge pile of socks is placed in the centre of the room and thoroughly jumbled up – there should be at least five or six pairs per player.

When everybody is ready, stand well back and switch off the lights. Players have two minutes to dive into the pile of socks and put as many of them on as possible. If any of your guests are the kind of low-down cheating types who would pull their gloves off as soon as the lights go out, you might want to substitute blindfolds all round for the darkened room.

At the end of the allotted time the lights go back on and players release each other's feet and disentangle their limbs as much as they feel inclined to. There are two ways to decide on a winner; you could go with the sheer number of socks worn, or favour the player who managed to pull on the most complete pairs.

A slightly more risqué version of this game involves a pile of women's knickers and men's underpants rather than socks but, unless you're the kind of person who has hundreds of pairs in a drawer (or habitually goes around stealing such items from washing lines), you might be hard pressed to find sufficient supplies of undies.

CRUMMOCK

Object of the game

To score goals while retaining your hat at all times.

What you need

Hats for all players, "bats" for all players and a "ball."

Another age-old and tremendously fun game for reducing levels of stress and stuffiness. Crummock is essentially a version of hockey but with the vital added ingredient of silliness. Basically, teams attempt to put the ball in their opponents' goal, but the equipment used should be as wacky as possible. Crummock bats could be rolled up umbrellas, plastic beach spades, inflatable bananas or a mixture of all three. The ball can be anything from an orange to a small cabbage.

The most important element of the game, however, is the wearing of hats. Headgear provided should be as large, ungainly and outlandish as possible. The one cast iron rule is that no player may touch the ball unless they are wearing a hat – it doesn't have to be the hat they started the game with, but it must recognizably be a hat worn on the head.

The tactics of hat-play are too complex to go into here but, essentially, it boils down to having players in your team that specialize in removing the hats of opposing team members by any means fair or foul. Whole minutes of play can go by with the ball all but forgotten as players wrestle with each other's head gear. Needless to say, this game requires a large, open space clear of breakables and impressionable children.

CROCODILES

Object of the game

For teams to race in the guise of crocodiles.

What you need

Lots of space.

How to play

This particular piece of silliness involves a straight race between two teams from point A to point B. The catch is that both teams must race in a rather ungainly chain that resembles a crocodile in every important detail save appearance, gait, speed and ferocity. To form a crocodile players squat on their heels in a line and place their hands on the shoulders, or around the waist, of the team member in front.

On the word "Go!" both crocodiles make for the finish line with as much speed and dignity as they can muster. Exactly how they move is a matter of trial and error since each member of the chain must remain in a squatting position. If at any point a team's crocodile comes unhinged, it must be reconnected in its entirety before that team can proceed. The winning crocodile is the first to get its tail across the line and should be rewarded with a tethered goat, represented by a sacrificed member of the losing team.

BALLOON COMBAT

Object of the game

To burst opponents' balloons while protecting your own.

What you need

String and a balloon and newspaper for every participant.

How to play

If you have understanding neighbours, and don't mind hosting a virtual riot in your house, this is an excellent way to work off pent-up aggression and form lasting enmities. Few party games have the potential for violence and injury provided by Balloon Combat so prepare to be amazed as the meekest of Marys becomes a bloodthirsty battlefield Valkyrie.

Competitors enter the arena equipped with a rolled up newspaper and with an inflated balloon tied securely to one ankle. The challenge is very simple – to burst other players' balloons while simultaneously defending your own. Balloons may only be burst by blows from rolled up newspapers; stepping on balloons or using concealed weapons such as keys is strictly prohibited and should be punished accordingly. The victor is the last warrior left standing with an intact balloon.

PEANUT PERIL

Object of the game

To transport a peanut while blindfolded.

What you need

A blindfold, peanuts and two pencils or similar short, straight sticks.

How to play

Another perilous balancing race that has competitors negotiating a short course while blindfolded. The peanut in peril should be gripped between two pencils held with arms outstretched at shoulder height. Spectators should take care not to wander into the path of oncoming competitors unless they wish to emulate the fate of King Harold at the Battle of Hastings.

The actual course can be as simple or complicated as you are prepared to make it, but should involve at least one or two turns to be negotiated – out of one room, along a corridor and into another room is a fair ready-made example.

Since competitors are blindfolded it's safer to have them racing against the clock than each other. The game can be played in teams, with the laurels going to the team with the smallest aggregate time, or as an elimination championship for individuals.

BOOBY TRAP

Object of the game

To avoid sitting on the chair with your name on it.

What you need

A chair, a cushion and one slip of paper for every player.

How to play

Like all the best games this one has very simple rules but involves lashings of strategy, bluff and cunning. The idea is to eliminate members of the opposing team by means of a booby-trapped chair before they can take you out using the same device. The most important skill in this game is the ability to keep a straight face when you realise that an opponent is about to be eradicated.

Divide players into two equal teams and have them sit facing each other across the room to foster a mood of mutual hatred and distrust. Place the chair of death in the middle of the room between the two teams and place the cushion on the chair. On separate slips of paper each team writes the names of each member of the opposing team – the slips must be identical to prevent the other team figuring out which slip has which name on it.

Whichever team is chosen to go first selects one slip of paper and places it on the chair, under the cushion, in such a manner that nobody on the other team can see which name has been chosen. The other team must now decide amongst themselves which of their number should risk sitting on the chair. If a player sits on the chair when it has his or her name on it, the attacking team gleefully bellow "Boom!" and that player is dead. If any other player sits on the chair, nothing happens except that the tension is raised by another notch. Play is passed from team to team until one or other is completely wiped out, the last player on a team going to meet his or her certain death with a tear in the eye and a song in the heart.

The booby trap only goes off when a player physically touches the cushion. It is perfectly legal for players to saunter over to the chair, and then change their minds at the last minute just to see what kind of a reaction this gets from the opposing team. To prevent things getting completely out of hand, introduce a time limit on decision making and insist that one or other player must take the chair when it has expired.

BLIND SQUIRRELS

Object of the game

To collect as many nuts as possible while blindfolded.

What you need

A blindfold for every player and lots of assorted nuts.

How to play

For spectators this one can provide top class entertainment as they watch grown men and women scrabbling around the floor like starving chipmunks. The idea is painfully simple. To gather as many nuts within five minutes as is possible while blindfolded and hampered by the frantic scurrying of other competitors.

To add a small element of skill use a variety of nuts, from almonds to Brazils, and award different points depending on their rarity in the playing environment. Provide players with paper bags to hold their hoards in case they attempt to store them in their cheeks. Numerous double-entendres along the lines of "Somebody keeps pinching my nuts!" are only to be expected.

BACK-TO-BACK

Object of the game

To win a race while encumbered by a partner walking backwards.

What you need

Lots of space.

How to play

A straightforward race with lots of physical contact that's good for forming partnerships. Form pairs with all the players in whichever way seems most fun, as long as it results in fairly evenly matched couples. Partners stand back-to-back at the starting line with arms linked. It's a good idea for the heavier or stronger partner to be facing down the course so that people don't get crushed when their partners fall backwards on top of them.

Couples can make their way to the finish line using any style that seems appropriate, but they must remain linked at all times. Teams that become uncoupled must return to the start. Depending on how much space is available the race can be a relay between teams of several couples or a straight free-for-all dash.

CARRY ON

Object of the game

To transport team members across the course using a variety of carrying techniques.

What you need

Lots of space.

How to play

Divide guests into two teams with equal numbers of men and women in both. In a display of old-fashioned chivalry the men have to carry the maidens across the room and back again without causing excessive injury or getting their faces slapped for inappropriately positioned hands.

The small but significant catch to all this is that no team can employ the same carrying method more than once. The first few carriers can get away with firemen's lifts, piggy backs and other conventional lifting techniques. Later on, more imagination will have to be employed, with a correspondingly greater risk of outrage on the part of those acting as baggage.

A variation of this game is for the women to carry the men.

ALL CHANGE

Object of the game

To put clothes on, and then take them off again, as rapidly as possible.

What you need

Two holdalls, two chairs, four nightdresses, four dressing gowns, four nightcaps and four pairs of slippers.

How to play

An excellent way to spot and bring out transvestite tendencies in your guests, this game relies on the age-old visual gag of men dressed up in women's clothing for its appeal. Bear in mind that items of clothing used in this game are likely to undergo some pretty rough handling so don't include your best silk nightdress.

Participants are divided into two teams of equal size and then each team forms itself into couples. Give the first couple in each team a holdall containing two nightdresses, two dressing gowns, two nightcaps and two pairs of slippers. Place the two chairs a good distance apart at the other end of the room.

At the off, each couple races to its chair and hurriedly unpacks its bag. Both partners must put on a nightdress, dressing gown, nightcap and slippers, aiding each other as they see fit, and then make one circuit of the chair before removing the nightclothes again, repacking their bag and racing back to hand the holdall to the next couple. The first team to get all its couples through this bizarre ritual wins the race.

More risqué versions of this game involve male players struggling to don skimpy knickers and bras while their female partners tangle with boxers and string vests. It's entirely up to you how much clothing they should be wearing to begin with.

SUIT SEARCH

Object of the game

To locate hidden playing cards.

What you need

Two packs of playing cards.

How to play

A nice, laid back team game that involves a minimum of rushing around. Players who employ a little brain power are likely to be more effective than those who hare around like maniacs. Before guests arrive, secrete all of the cards from one pack around the house. They should be difficult to spot, but not so well concealed that people are going to start taking up the carpets to find them.

When all players are assembled, divide them into equal teams and give each team member a different card from the second, well-shuffled, pack. Each player has the simple task of locating the twin of his or her card and returning it to the host, who issues another card to be matched. The clever player will make a mental note of any other cards that they come across on their travels and pass that information on to team mates. The team with the most retrieved cards at the end of the thirty-minute time limit can claim victory.

A rather obvious method of cheating at this game is to simply pocket any card that you come across thereby ensuring that nobody on the other team can find it and that you will always know where it is should the need arise. Short of requiring guests to play stark naked there is little a host can do about this. It all depends on what you value more, honest game play or nudity taboos.

SUCKERS

Object of the game

To transport peas by suction power.

What you need

Dried peas, drinking straws, saucers and a large bowl.

How to play

Another game that will test the lung capacity of your guests to the limits. Before proceeding any further ensure that the dried peas or beans that you have chosen will not under any circumstances fit through the drinking straws — sucking a dried pea at high velocity into the back of your throat is an excellent way to choke to death.

Divide players into teams of two and give each pair a drinking straw each. Place the large bowl at one end of the room and fill it with the dried peas. For each pair that is playing there must be a saucer half way down the room, and another at the far end of the room.

The first player of each pair takes up position near the bowl of peas, and on the word "Go!" must lift out a pea by sucking it through the straw. Keeping the pea affixed to the end of his straw, he must transport it to his team's saucer and carefully drop it in. His team mate then takes over and carries the pea in the same manner to their saucer at the far end of the room. The pair that manages to transport the largest number of peas the full length of the room within the allotted time wins the game.

Peas that are dropped on the floor, or that bounce out of saucers, must stay where they are and don't count towards a team's score. Causing people to laugh so that they blow instead of suck is a legal, if slightly hazardous, tactic.

BREAKFAST IS SERVED

Object of the game

To race with a precariously balanced tennis ball.

What you need

Two plastic plates and two tennis balls.

How to play

There is nothing like a game of skill and subtlety to enthral the average party-goer, and this is nothing like a game of skill and subtlety – its more a question of staggering about and blind luck.

Any guest who has ever worked as a waiter will be able to empathize fully with the ordeal of his team mates in this quirky little racing jaunt.

Divide players into two equal teams and stand them in rows. Team members should space themselves out equally by placing a hand on the shoulder of the player in front and shuffling back until their arms are straight. The first player in the line receives a plastic plate, which he holds on an outstretched palm, and a tennis ball, which must be balanced on the plate.

At the word "Go!" the tennis-ball bearing waiters must weave their way through the line of their team mates and back again without dropping their tennis balls. On returning to his or her starting position the waiter hands the plate and ball to the next player in line and rushes around to joint the back of the queue so that it remains the same length. The relay continues until all members of a team have made the slalom run. Dropped tennis balls result in the guilty waiter going back to the beginning of the run and trying again.

If playing outside you might want to consider using full soup bowls balanced on trays (spills being refilled from a bowl of water) or some other potentially messy cargo for the waiters to carry.

PEG DROP

Object of the game

To drop pegs into empty milk bottles.

What you need

One empty milk bottle and twelve clothes pegs for every four players.

How to play

A game to test physical skill without straining muscles, peg dropping is an ancient game with roots stretching back as far as the invention of the peg – or the milk bottle, depending on how you want to look at it. Either way, it's bound to become an Olympic event before long, so now's the time to get some practice in.

Divide guests into teams of three or four and give each team a milk bottle and twelve pegs. According to ancient peg-dropping lore, each team member takes it in turns to attempt to drop his share of the team's pegs into their bottle.

The peg-dropping position is as follows: stand upright with feet together and toes just touching the milk bottle, the peg must be held between thumb and forefinger and dropped from exactly nose height. Stooping, bending, crouching or any other method of bringing nose and bottle into closer proximity are strictly forbidden. Pegs that miss their mark must remain where they are and the honours go to the team with the most pegs in their bottle when the dust settles.

WAFER WHISTLING

Object of the game

To eat a dry wafer as swiftly as possible and then manage to whistle.

What you need

One chair and one dry wafer for each player.

How to play

Divide players into two equal teams and position them on opposite sides of the room. Put two rows of chairs, one chair for each team member, back-to-back in the middle of the room. Place one wafer, cracker, water biscuit or similar dry and flaky edible morsel on the seat of each chair.

On the whistle, the first player of each team rushes over to the first chair in the line, seizes his biscuit, sits down and proceeds to eat it as quickly as possible. Once the biscuit has been wholly and verifiably put beyond use, he or she must produce an audible whistle – it doesn't have to be a rendition of Beethoven's Fifth, but it must be a recognizable whistle. With this done to the satisfaction of the referee, player one rushes back to his or her team and tags the next team member.

The first team in which all members complete this travesty of entertainment wins the contest. Referees may want to consider wearing goggles to ward off high-velocity wafer fragments.

WITCH HUNT

Object of the game

To find the witch before she turns you to stone.

What you need

A torch (optional).

How to play

An excuse for adults to play hide and seek and re-enact medieval witch hunts at the same time. Choose one player to be the witch and, if the fancy takes you, equip them with a cloak, pointy hat and stick-on warts. All the other players are fearful and ignorant yokels.

Give the witch a set time to find a hiding place, then turn off all the lights and set the pitchfork-wielding villagers off in cautious pursuit. Searchers are allowed to call out "Where are you witch?" in suitably peasant-like tones to which the witch must reply with an eerie cackle, but they can only do this twice. The witch is free to move around if she chooses. Whoever succeeds in finding the witch dons the pointy hat for the next round.

A cunning variation of this game has the witch equipped with a magical torch that she can use to turn hapless villagers into stone by flashing it in their eyes. Any villager petrified in this manner must stay standing where they are until the game is over, or until they get bored and wander off to the kitchen for another drink.

Use any available method to make the game as spooky as possible, but you should probably stop short of burning at the stake or ordeals by drowning!

TELEGRAM!

Object of the game

To disrupt the postal system.

What you need

A blindfold and pen and paper for the referee.

How to play

An unholy union of Blind Man's Buff and the Royal Mail this game provides a horrifying insight into the kind of misfortune that can befall an urgently anticipated cheque lost in the post.

As with certain other forms of Blind Man's Buff, players form a circle with whoever is chosen to go first standing in the middle and sporting a blindfold. Go around the circle of players and have each one call out the name of a different town. Make a note of the town called out by each player.

Once all preparations are complete it's up to the referee to call out the origin and destination of the first piece of mail. Pick two of the towns named by players and say "The mail is going from Basingstoke to Bedford" or whatever. The two players who named these towns must immediately rush across the circle and take up each other's positions in the ring without being tagged by the blind post master in the middle.

Players stay in the centre of the circle until they catch someone to take their place. At any point the referee may shout out "Telegram!" and unleash pandemonium as every player must rush to a position on the opposite side of the circle.

WATER BOMBS

Object of the game

To avoid being soaked by water-filled balloons.

What you need

Several water-filled balloons.

How to play

This is definitely one for the garden, preferably in the height of summer when a soaking will come as more of a welcome relief than a potential health risk. Essentially, this is a game of catch, where the risks of fumbling are obvious. You can make the rules as complex or simple as desired, either way the whole affair is likely to descend into an orgy of mutual irrigation.

Divide players into equal teams and pass out as many water-filled balloons as you can be bothered to prepare. Team mates must gently toss the balloons to each other around a circle. Dropping a balloon, or allowing it to burst all over you, results in elimination.

Continue until all balloons are burst, or all but one player from a team is eliminated. It would be wise for players to wear swimming costumes underneath their clothes.

HOPPING MAD

Object of the game

To hop around an assault course while balancing an orange on a spoon.

What you need

One orange and one spoon for each competitor, some chairs and some string.

How to play

Although it sounds fairly simple this game involves one of the most fiendishly difficult challenges known to man – right up there with keeping New Year's resolutions. To prepare you will need to lay out a circular race course that includes a couple of jumps. Construct jumps by tying a length of string between two chairs so that it forms a bar about eighteen inches off the ground.

Guests bonkers enough to compete should be issued with the time-honoured spoon and orange combo. Line up as many runners as your course can uncomfortably accommodate at the start line and signal the start.

At the off, players must hop around the course, negotiating the jumps, while keeping the orange balanced in the spoon. Dropped oranges must be retrieved with the spoon while the guilty party is still balanced on one leg. Needless to say, it could take some time to complete a race, especially when competitors indulge in the usual practice of sabotaging their opponents.

FOUR-LEGGED RACE

Object of the game

To race with your legs strapped to your team mates.

What you need

Lots of space and some strong cords.

How to play

This is of course a cunning variation of the old sports day favourite the three-legged race. In this version, three competitors are strapped together at the shins to form a lumbering and amusingly uncoordinated monster. Note that strapping team mates together at the shins results in far fewer sprained and twisted joints than joining them at the ankles.

Give competitors some time to figure out a way of walking before starting the race and then line them up for the off. Since it is practically impossible to get up if you fall in this configuration, teams should be allowed to cross the line by any means they can manage, as long as they are still fastened together.

TRUE OR FALSE

Object of the game

To race for a chair depending on the answer to a question.

What you need

Two chairs and a set of pre-prepared statements.

How to play

This game tests intellectual skills and the ability to tear across a room at high speed – an admirable and rare combination of talents in any gathering of friends. Before guests arrive you will need to prepare a set of statements that are "True" or "False." Quiz books and other commercial trivia games are a good source of statements – you just have to alter the questions into a true or false format.

Assemble all guests and divide them into two equal teams. Position the teams on opposite sides of the room and then place one chair at either end of the room between the two teams. Assign one of these chairs the "True" chair and the other the "False" chair. Make sure everybody is clear about which chair is which to avoid arguments later – if necessary a put a sign on each.

The first player from each team stands up and they both position themselves in the centre of the room equidistant from the two chairs. On hearing the first statement they must decide if it is true or false and rush to sit down on the corresponding chair. If both players make for the same chair, the first to sit down gets the point (assuming it's the correct chair of course). Tot up the scores once every player from each team has had a go and then declare the winner.

As an interesting variation, this game could be played with statements about guests themselves. You will need to collect secret revelations from each guest and mix in an equal number of false ones of your own devising. Obviously you shouldn't use statements that are about the players participating in that round.

STEPPING STONES

Object of the game

To cross the room using moveable stepping stones.

What you need

Two shoe boxes or two small cushions for each team and two lengths of rope or cord.

How to play

Lay out the two lengths of rope on the ground to serve as the banks of your river, they should be at least twelve feet apart. Divide players into two equal teams and put half of the members of each team on one bank of the river and half on the other (it doesn't have to be exactly half if there are an odd number of players in the teams).

To cross the river team members must use the shoe boxes as stepping stones. The first player from each team tosses one of the boxes a little way into the river and steps into it with one foot. Standing on one leg, he or she then tosses the other box a bit further forward and steps into it with the other foot. Utilizing every ounce of agility and balance that he or she can muster the player must then retrieve the first box and drop it a little further forward to make progress across the river.

With the first team member safely across, the stepping stones are used by the next to transfer him or her to the opposite bank. The first team to get all its members onto the opposite bank from the one they started on wins the game. Falling into the river means returning to the bank you started from and trying again.

Players will quickly learn that small steps are usually more profitable than giant strides if they want to avoid strained groins and the embarrassment of split trousers. Bear in mind that shoe boxes can be quite slippery on carpeted floors, so you might want to use small cushions instead.

TOWER OF BABEL

Object of the game

To build a balanced tower out of cups and plates.

What you need

Lots of disposable or unbreakable plastic cups and plates.

How to play

A challenge requiring nerves of steel and a steady hand, both of which should be in short supply if the wine has been flowing steadily. Expect chaos as plastic cups and plates rain down in the fallout of each spectacular tower collapse.

Place lots of plastic cups of the same size on a table at one end of the room, and lots of plastic plates on another table at the other end of the room. Starting at one table or the other, players must cross the room repeatedly to gather the materials to build a tower of plates and cups that they must carry with them. Towers must be constructed of alternate cups and plates, but players can choose to begin with a plate or a cup. Competitors may only hold the bottom element of their tower to keep it balanced.

Although it's great fun, deliberately knocking down other people's towers as they pass by should be discouraged. Left unchecked, this kind of behaviour tends to lead to open combat among guests using plastic cups and plates as weapons.

HUNT THE THIMBLE

Object of the game

To spot the location of a hidden thimble.

What you need

A thimble or other small object.

How to play

This is one of the all-time classic party games – simple, yet effective, entertainment. Unlike other searching games, this one has the advantage of involving everybody because the object of the game is just to spot the thimble, not to jump up and down triumphantly while pointing it out to other players.

One person is chosen to be the first thimble-hider and everyone else leaves the room. Within a time limit of about a minute the thimble-hider must place the thimble somewhere in the room so that it's visible but difficult to spot. Once this is done, the searchers are called back in and wander around looking for the elusive thimble. The key rule to grasp is that, when a player spots the thimble, he or she should just go and quietly sit down. To ensure they don't give its position away to other guests, a player should wander around a bit, pretending to continue the search, before returning to his or her seat.

The game continues until all players have spotted the thimble or until only one player is left and the others take pity. Usually, the last player to sit down becomes the thimble-hider for the next round, but that honour could equally go to the first. Needless to say, this game doesn't have to be played with a thimble. Any small and discreet object, such as a small battery or a coin could be used, as long as players know what they are looking for.

FRANTIC FEATHERS

Object of the game

To keep a feather airborne using breath power alone.

What you need

A small feather for every team.

How to play

A game guaranteed to get everyone light headed and giggly. Played in teams of three or four the challenge is to blow a feather across a room and land it on a target table or chair. Teams should start in different positions around the edges of the room and the target should be placed in the centre.

Feathers may only be kept aloft by lung power, illegally trans-porting feathers on heads, shoulders or any other part of the body should be punished with a back-to-start penalty. Inadvertently sucking in feathers and swallowing them is also contrary to the rules, but there's not a lot that can be done about it short of a complex surgical procedure.

The fun really starts as each team begins to converge on the same area and opportunities to blow competitors' feathers off course start to present themselves. If at all possible it's a good idea to give each team a different coloured feather to prevent the evil practice of feather hijacking.

STOICS

Object of the game

To avoid smiling or laughing.

What you need

No equipment necessary but amusing headgear could be used.

How to play

Games in which smiling, laughing or showing any signs of jollity are forbidden are of course the very games most likely to cause plenty of each, and this is a classic example. The game begins with all players sitting cross-legged on the floor in a circle. At a given signal smiling, snickering, grinning, giggling and guffawing become illegal. Most players immediately crack-up at this point, so you'll probably have to allow a settling-down period before play begins in earnest.

The first player turns to the person seated on his or her left and nudges or tweaks them in a fairly minor manner – a quick poke in the upper arm would be perfect for starters. That player must then turn to his or her left and perform exactly the same action on the next player. This continues all the way around the circle until it gets back to the first player who takes his or her poke and then thinks of another action to pass on.

As the game progresses the provocations should escalate from nudges to funny-face pulling to outright tickling – passing an amusing hat, or similar embarrassing apparel, around the circle is also an option. Any player who cracks a grin is immediately disqualified. Most players rarely last the first round, especially if they are sitting a fair way around the circle and have plenty of time to anticipate the coming provocation.

SPOON-FED

Object of the game

To consume foul tasting foods in the fastest time.

What you need

Teaspoons, pickled onion, cloves of garlic, peppers or any other hard-to-swallow foodstuffs.

How to play

Playing this game can seriously damage the quality of your breath and should not be attempted prior to any other games that require close, personal contact. Exactly what foods you choose should depend on the bravado and personal tastes of your guests – some people actually like pickled onions – but raw cloves of garlic and hot chilli peppers are usually sufficiently challenging for most palates.

The rules are very simple. Players are arranged into equal teams and given a teaspoon and a bowl of the chosen foodstuff each. Player one feeds two teaspoons full to player two, who must completely consume their contents, before taking spoon and bowl and feeding the same to player three. A team completes the task when the last player feeds the first.

ALL THE WORLD'S A STAGE

Given the right conditions, and a glass or two of inhibition softener, everyone can find their inner thespian. The games in this dramatically inclined section are unlikely to produce Oscar winning performances, but they're guaranteed to have you rolling in the isles. Even De Niro had to start somewhere.

ON BENDED KNEE

Object of the game

To propose in the most heart-warming and flattering way possible.

What you need

No special equipment needed.

How to play

An excellent game for stirring up jealousy and ill-feeling at a party where things are becoming too comfortable and boring. Play this game too often and you might find divorce lawyers clamouring to leave their cards scattered discreetly about your house.

The game is simplicity itself, getting through it without causing offence is another matter entirely. Participants write their names on slips of paper and place them in a hat. Depending on preference the men's names should go in a separate hat from the women's, or you can have them all together.

Players take it in turns to draw a name from the hat (if it's their own name, they put it back and draw another). The challenge is to stage a convincing proposal of marriage to the person whose name is on the slip of paper. This can be a liberating experience if you happen to draw the name of someone you've always fancied, although care should be taken not to be too convincing if your current partner happens to be watching.

Award a two-week honeymoon in Barbados to the most convincing, or amusing, pair.

CHARADES

Object of the game

To guess the title being mimed by your team mate.

What you need

A list of film, song, theatre, book and television programme titles.

How to play

A party just isn't a party unless someone suggests a game of Charades – whether anyone agrees to it or not is another matter. Charades has unfairly gained a reputation as a bit of a tedious pastime. Given the right group of people and a willingness to throw body and soul into the game, however, it can be one of the most entertaining and accessible party activities.

The game can be played in two teams or as an individual challenge, depending on how competitive you feel. In both cases, it's far better if the host has pre-prepared a set of cards or slips of paper with film, book, and TV titles on them for players to pick at random. In the individual game, the player who guesses correctly becomes the next mime. In a team game a time limit of about two minutes should be set before the chance to guess is passed over to the other side.

Mimed performances must be completely silent, but there are a number of accepted hand signals that can be used to speed-up the process:

It's a film – The left hand forms an eyepiece while the right hand cranks an imaginary movie camera.

It's a play – Both hands are swept downwards to represent curtains.

It's a TV programme – A square is drawn in the air by both forefingers.

It's a song – One hand is placed over the heart while the other is outstretched in the pose of an old-fashioned crooner.

It's a book – Both hands are clasped together and then opened out like the covers of a book.

Number of words – The relevant number of fingers are held up.

Word being mimed – The relevant number of fingers are held up.

Number of syllables – The relevant number of syllables are tapped on the forearm.

Sounds like – An earlobe is gently tugged.

A short word – Forefinger and thumb are held close together until somebody calls out the correct short word (at, in, of, an, etcetera).

The word "The" – One forefinger is held upright while the other is placed on top to form a capital "T."

A close guess – The forefinger of one hand is placed on the nose while the other forefinger is pointed at the person who made the guess.

Whole thing – A large circle is described in the air.

The game can also be played using phrases, proverbs or ordinary words if you prefer.

SHADOWS

Object of the game

To guess a scene being acted out by team mates.

What you need

A large white sheet and a strong lamp.

How to play

This game takes some preparation but, if done well, the results can be quite spectacular. An excellent game for aspiring actors or others who take their theatre seriously.

Set up a large white sheet so that it forms a screen near one end of the room. Place a bright light some distance behind the screen so that a person standing between the light and the screen casts a crisp and relatively undistorted shadow visible from the other side of the sheet. Next, devise a series of scenarios that two people can act out. They can be as innocent as buying a pint at the bar or as saucy as Bill Clinton interviewing Monica Lewinsky. Alternatively, proverbs, nursery rhymes or well-known scenes from movies could be selected.

Players should be divided into small teams of three or four members each. At the start of each round, two members of a team come forward and are given a scenario to be acted out. The acting is of course done behind the screen, so players should bear in mind that it's all about large gestures and poses rather than subtle facial expressions. Team mates of the acting pair have a minute to decide what scene they are seeing, and may have as many guesses as they want in that time. If they fail to guess correctly, it's thrown open to the other teams.

Keep the performances going until there are no more scenarios left. The team that guessed correctly most often wins the game. To really get into the spirit of things it's nice to have a box of generic props that actors can select and use as they see fit.

MUTANT SUPERHEROES

Object of the game

To guess the name of the mutant superhero.

What you need

No special equipment needed.

How to play

A game of pure imagination requiring considerable acting ability and presence of mind on the part of players. Alternatively, a silly farce requiring only that players have had enough wine to loosen their inhibitions.

Participants take it in turns to assume the identities of awesome superheroes. However, these are no ordinary superheroes. Batman, Superman and Spiderman are not invited. These are superheroes created by freak accidents involving high doses of radiation and ordinary household objects such as irons, toasters and tubs of margarine.

Players attempt to convey their identities by acting in character as their chosen superhero. They are allowed to speak and answer questions, but must not identify themselves or give direct clues. For example, Low Fat Spread Man is allowed to boast of his abilities to lower your cholesterol and may hint at his origins in the chilled-goods section of a local supermarket, but he cannot directly mention low-fat spread or say, "I'm something to do with what you spread on your toast."

The most convincing and entertaining superhero should be given a prize, and a small red cape to wear for the rest of the evening.

ALIBIS

Object of the game

To construct a watertight alibi.

What you need

No special equipment needed.

How to play

For fans of whodunits and TV detectives that fancy themselves as CID detectives, this is an opportunity to display their skills of interrogation and deductive reasoning (no police brutality please). For those contemplating committing a major crime, an opportunity to practice their lying techniques.

Divide players into criminal gangs of two members each and assign each couple a crime that they must provide an alibi for. The nature of the crime doesn't really mater, as long as its heinous and blood-curdling, but the time period does. Teams are required to account for their movements during a two-hour period on a particular day. Send the first pair of criminal masterminds out of the room and give them five minutes in which to come up with a convincing story that accounts for both of them during the period in question.

After five minutes the first team member is dragged in to help police with their inquiries while the other waits nervously outside chain smoking and drinking endless cups of vending-machine coffee. The detectives, namely the other players, have five or ten minutes in which to interview the first suspect. They should try to ascertain as much detail as possible as to where the suspect was at the time of the crime, what they were doing and who they were with. Notes may be taken if you wish to allow it.

Once the first player has been sucked dry of information, the second is wheeled in. With Gestapo-like efficiency the detectives attempt to turn up some vital discrepancy between the answers given by the first suspect and those given by the second. If the host agrees that conclusive proof of lying has been uncovered, the first pair are considered well and truly nicked.

Continue the game until all pairs have had a turn as suspects and award an eight-to-ten stretch in Pentonville to the most convincing liars.

INSTANT PANTOMIME

Object of the game

To perform a pantomime using random props.

What you need

A collection of odd props.

How to play

Ugly sisters, shrinking Cinderallas, sleeping beauties and other unfulfilled panto performers should get a real kick out of this game. Before play begins the host will need to assemble a box of props, three of which will be used in each performance. Suitable objects might include fairly obvious items such as outrageous wigs and headgear as well as more off-the-wall offerings such as kitchen implements, rubber ducks, amusingly shaped vegetables and dusty relics from the attic.

Divide players into teams of three or four, assign three props to each team and allow five or ten minutes to come up with a pantomime scene that makes full use of the equipment made available to them. The same props can be assigned to more than one team, since only one team will be performing at a time.

Stage the instant pantomimes at one end of the room and provide other players with rotten fruit to throw. If there really must be a winner, give points for the number of "He's behind you!" or "Oh, no he isn't!" cries generated by performers.

CHINESE MIMES

Object of the game

To pass a mime performance from team member to team member.

What you need

No special equipment needed.

How to play

Chinese Whispers without speaking may sound like a pretty dumb idea, but when you realise that the whispering is replaced by miming, the comical potential becomes obvious.

Players are split into two fairly equal teams and one team is sent to languish in the next room. Teams should establish a running order before play begins by numbering their members consecutively.

With one team out of the way, the other comes up with a simple situation to be mimed by the opposition. It can be anything from extracting ketchup from a bottle to conducting a full body-cavity search. Player one from the opposing team is then called in and told what he or she has to mime. After the shock has worn off, player one calls in player two and performs the mime. At no point must players in the miming team communicate verbally to one another.

Once player two has seen and marvelled at the mime of their team mate, player three is called in and player two has to repeat the mime as accurately as they can remember. Player three then performs to player four and so on until the last player has seen the mime and is left with the well nigh impossible task of guessing what the original scenario suggested by the opposing team was.

Continue play until both teams have had three or four turns at miming – it's a good idea if teams are allowed to change their running order each round otherwise the same player is left with having to guess and never gets to perform.

WORST IN THE WORLD

Object of the game

To act like the world's worst whatever.

What you need

No special equipment needed.

How to play

A game for people with no ambition. Players are required to act like the most hopeless, clueless, brainless individuals they possible can – not a stretch in some cases. Before the game, prepare a list of world's worsts. Examples might include the world's worst kisser, the world's worst hairdresser, the world's worst arachnophobe or the world's worst taxi-hailer. Write these on slips of paper and put them in whatever you like to pretend is a hat.

To play, performers draw a slip of paper each and attempt to act as if they were the person it describes. Performances must be silent and pointing at other guests, to demonstrate the world's worst lover for instance, is strictly disallowed.

THE RAILWAY CARRIAGE GAME

Object of the game

To prevent your opponent from using their secret phrase.

What you need

Two chairs.

How to play

Place the two chairs facing each other in the centre of the room and imagine that they represent two seats in a railway carriage travelling through occupied territory in 1941. Players should be equipped with trench coats and trilbies to complete the picture, but this isn't strictly necessary. Suspicious SS officers wishing players good luck in heavily accented tones are also purely optional.

Before each pair of players board the carriage and take their seats they should both be equipped with a secret phrase that they must attempt to slip into the ensuing conversation. Players shouldn't know each other's secret phrase. As the conversation progresses each player must try and steer it so that they can use their secret phrase as if it were a normal part of the conversation – players aren't simply allowed to blurt out their phrases since this leads to instant arrest and incarceration in Colditz.

Secret phrases should be made as bizarre and unlikely as possible. "Do you have a light?" is no good, "My uncle once visited Beijing," is more along the right lines and "I haven't had my ears syringed since 1936," is perfect. As well as trying to sneak their own phrase into the conversation, each spy must attempt to prevent their opponents from using theirs by spotting trends in the conversation. Players who are judged to have used their phrases out of context are eliminated, otherwise the first player to plausibly introduce their phrase into the conversation wins the round.

SPLIT PERSONALITIES

Object of the game

To dress like one character but behave like another.

What you need

A fancy dress party.

How to play

Fancy dress parties are perennially popular and this game gives guests the opportunity to adopt not one but two alternative identities – any psychiatrists present should have a field day.

This game can only be played at a fancy dress party where guests have been forewarned since it requires them to arrive "in character." The idea is for players to dress as one character, but to behave as a completely different one. So, for example, it's perfectly possible to meet a guest dressed as Long John Silver who behaves like Dame Edna Everage.

At the end of the evening, or at some other point in the proceedings, participants are invited to guess who other players have been impersonating.

UNLIMITED QUESTIONS

Object of the game

To answer questions with more questions.

What you need

No special equipment needed.

How to play

Played in pairs this game encourages the annoying habit of answering questions with other questions. One player starts the ball rolling by asking the other a simple question such as "How did you get here tonight?" to which his opponent might reply "Why, are you looking for a lift home?" inviting the retaliation "Do I look like the kind of person who would accept lifts from perfect strangers?"

Play continues in this fashion until one or other player is unable to think of a question within a reasonable time limit or makes the mistake of answering with a statement. Adjudicators should be on the look out for repeated questions to prevent an endless ping-pong round of "What did you say?" or "Why do you ask?" type responses.

Hosts should be warned that these conversations almost inevitably become acrimonious after a short period of time.

ADVERBS

Object of the game

To perform mimes in the manner described by an adverb.

What you need

No special equipment needed.

How to play

An adverb, for anyone who wasn't paying attention in English classes, is a word that describes a verb. Examples would include happily, slowly, gently and carelessly.

Send one player out of the room while those remaining choose an adverb – make sure everybody knows what the adverb is. When the player returns he or she can ask any other player to perform a simple mime in the manner of the secret adverb. The guesser can ask up to four people to perform mimes – not necessarily the same mime for each one. Examples might include "Tie your shoelaces in the manner of the adverb," "Ride a bicycle in the manner of the adverb," or "Kiss your wife in the manner of the adverb." Mimers proceed to tie their shoelaces in a lascivious manner, or whatever is appropriate.

Players who fail to guess correctly after their four chances are eliminated. Successful guessers get another go. The player that guesses the most adverbs wins the game.

CONVERSATION STOPPERS

Object of the game

To prevent other players from continuing the conversation.

What you need

No special equipment required.

How to play

Conversations are conducted by groups of three or four players. One player starts the ball rolling with a simple observation such as "This is a terrible party, isn't it." The next player must continue the conversation in a normal manner, but the first word of his or her sentence must begin with the last letter of the previous player's last word – "T" in this case.

As the name of the game suggests, the goal is to stop the conversation by leaving the next player with tricky letters such as "X" or "Z" to begin their comments with. Players who are unable to contribute something intelligible within about ten seconds should be eliminated. Continue until just one player remains in each group and pit the winners against each other in a grand final.

A MILLION DIFFERENT USES

Object of the game

To find as many different uses as possible for an object.

What you need

A selection of odd and inspiring props.

How to play

The key to this game is to provide sufficiently bizarre props for players to perform with. Sink plungers, traffic cones (legally purchased from the proper authorities of course), oddly shaped pieces of pottery and arcane garden implements are all possible candidates.

Given an object each, performers have to come up with as many plausible uses for it as they can possibly imagine. Play passes from performer to performer until the well of inspiration runs dry. Rounds of applause go to the most, or the most amusing, uses acted out by performers.

BEGINNING, MIDDLE AND END

Object of the game

To devise a short theatrical piece.

What you need

No special equipment needed, but props may be provided.

How to play

This really is a game for thespians only since it requires an entire theatrical piece to be put together in less time than it takes to brew a decent pot of coffee. The host is required to provide three lines of dialogue or stage directions that mark the beginning, middle and end of each playlet. For maximum comic effect these should be as farcical as possible. An example might be something along the lines of:

Beginning: "Erica, I almost didn't recognize you without your rubber gloves on!"

Middle: He falls to his knees sobbing for forgiveness.

End: "Trust me, I wouldn't go in there for a while."

Give each team ten minutes or so in separate rooms to work the lines provided into a coherent story. Teams can be provided with different beginnings, middles and ends, but the results are some- times more interesting when everybody is working with the same material. Present the finished plays and award Golden Globes for the most heart-wrenching performances.

BAR CRAWL

Object of the game

To discover what kind of establishment you have wandered into.

What you need

No special equipment.

How to play

Anyone who has wandered into a pub and spent an hour merrily chatting away to the locals before it dawned on them that everybody present appeared to be of the same sex or attired in unusually figure-hugging rubber garments should recognise the premise of this game at once.

The idea is that one hapless player has wandered into a bar frequented exclusively by one type of customer. By conversing with the other players he must figure out if he's stumbled into a gathering of lawyers, or cannibals, or rock musicians or whatever.

One player is selected to leave the room while the others settle on a theme for the bar. This doesn't have to be restricted to a profession or sexual preference but could extend to, for example, people who only answer questions truthfully if they are put to them by members of the same sex, or people who are obsessed by shoe sizes or people with a pathological fear of the colour purple.

The interloper may asks questions freely but regulars cannot directly answer inquiries such as "What is your profession?" or "What are you most afraid of?" to influence the mystery. Each player takes turn as gatecrasher, but there are no winners.

JUST A MINUTE

Object of the game

To speak for a full minute on a given subject.

What you need

A list of subjects and a stopwatch.

How to play

Just a Minute has been an immensely popular feature on Radio 4 for years and the game itself was played more than a hundred years ago by the Victorians, so there must be something in it.

Each player attempts to speak on a subject chosen by the host for one minute without committing the sins of hesitation, repetition or deviation. While one player is speaking, any other player may challenge them for infractions of these rules and the clock is stopped until the matter is resolved.

Hesitation, fairly obviously, is a failure to keep up a smooth and constant dialogue or resorting too frequently to "Ums" and "Ahs." Repetition strictly refers to repeating the same piece of information but could also be applied to the repeated use of a word. Deviation just means straying too far from the subject.

Any player who mounts a successful challenge takes over the subject for whatever period of time remains on the clock, or until they are themselves successfully challenged. Completing a full minute is an extremely rare and difficult achievement and should be rewarded with five points. Being the player speaking when the minute is up is less difficult and should only garner two points. Successful challenges earn one point and unsuccessful challenges cost a point.

Players who don't feel they are up to the considerable challenge of a round of Just a Minute might want to consider its sister games Just Half a Minute and Just Fifteen Seconds.

EMOTIONAL INVOLVEMENT

Object of the game

To mime emotions.

What you need

No special equipment needed.

How to play

Prepare a list of emotions for players to draw from a hat and prepare for an experience both harrowing and uplifting as guests mime anything from terror, to lust, to beatitude. Mimes, being mimes, may not include sound of any kind. Other players attempt to guess the precise emotion being portrayed.

For students of human psychology the game could be adapted so that mimes are required to portray the emotion they feel best characterizes one of the other guests. Other players have to identify the person as well as the emotion in this case.

STRIKE A POSE

Object of the game

To convey an adjective with a pose.

What you need

No special equipment needed.

How to play

Write a selection of adjectives on slips of paper and put them in whatever you like to pretend is a hat. The adjectives should be actable so "Purple" is no good, unless you have a quantity of purple body paint to hand. Examples could include amazed, undecided, slovenly, evil or sly.

Players take it in turns to draw a slip of paper from the hat-substitute and strike a motionless pose that is intended to convey the adjective written on it. Posers must remain absolutely still for at least thirty seconds without cracking up and are not allowed to speak or give any other audible clues.

Plaudits go to the player who manages to strike the most expressive pose, or who manages to convey a seemingly impossible adjective such as "Talented."

GUESS WHO

Object of the game

To identify and impersonate a famous person.

What you need

No special equipment needed.

How to play

A fairly straightforward guessing game with a couple of tricky variations that can be used to catch players unawares. Banish one person from the room while the others think of a celebrity, alive or dead, real or fictitious. By the same bizarre magical processes that underlie a great many party games, the person outside the room is assumed to have taken on the identity of the famous person selected by the others, but to have lost his or her memory at the same time.

On re-entering the room, the single player attempts to ascertain his or her identity by asking other guests simple question along the lines of "Am I male?" or "Am I dead?" Questions can only be answered "Yes" or "No." After a maximum of three questions have been put to each player the guesser must do an impersonation of the celebrity that he thinks was chosen. If you simply must have winners and losers, award one point for a correct impersonation, two points if it's a particularly good one, and subtract a point if it's completely on the wrong track.

If you are playing with people who are already familiar with the game, try one of these underhanded tricks to confuse them into submission. In one variation players don't have a particular celebrity in mind but answer questions according to the way they are put. An example might be for female players to always answer "Yes" and male players to always answer "No." A second variation requires players to answer questions as if they were about the person sitting on their right, rather than about a celebrity. In both cases the guesser will be thoroughly confused but will nevertheless attempt to impersonate somebody or other.

A BIT OF PEACE

Parties are about fun, but that doesn't necessarily mean you have to spend the entire evening racing about with rolled up newspapers or hiding in cupboards. When guests start passing out from their exertions, or when your carpets have taken enough wear and tear for one evening, sit everyone down and take a breather with a game that demands little of brains or bodies.

EDITORS

Object of the game

To re-assemble a newspaper article.

What you need

Newspaper articles.

How to play

For budding newspaper editors, this game requires players to make sense of lines from a newspaper article jumbled into a meaningless mess. For some newspapers this might be easier than for others, especially those in which the articles are habitually meaningless messes to start with.

To prepare you will need to select a short article between a hundred and two hundred words in length. Television review pages are a good source. Cut the article into its constituent sentences – it's a good idea to enlarge the text with a photocopier to make the cutting up job less fiddly – and spread them out on a board or tray. You will need one cut-up article for every pair of players.

Couples have a set time in which to arrange the fragmented sentences into the correct order – about five minutes should be plenty, depending on the length of the article. The pair with the most accurate re-assembly wins the game.

MISSING LETTERS

Object of the game

To avoid using a certain letter of the alphabet.

What you need

No special equipment.

How to play

Divide players into two teams of equal size and have them sitting within earshot of each other. A letter of the alphabet must be chosen as taboo – this could be done by drawing a Scrabble tile from a bag. Bear in mind that some letters are a lot harder to avoid using then others, vowels for example should almost certainly be exempt. Equally, some letters are far too easy to avoid, "Z" and "X" being obvious examples.

Once a taboo letter has been chosen, team members take it in turns to ask their opposite numbers questions in an attempt to get them to use the forbidden letter in their answers. So, if the taboo letter happened to be "K" for example, the first player on one team could ask the first player on the opposing team "Where do you keep your dishwasher?" hoping to make him say "In the kitchen." His opponent must answer the question in an intelligible way but, in this case, could easily escape by replying "Next to the fridge."

To give players time to think of sneaky questions the order of play should pass from player one on the first team to player one on the second team to player two on the first team and so on until everybody has asked one question. Using the taboo letter in an answer (it's fine to use it in a question) results in a point scored for the team that asked the question. Set a maximum of twenty questions per team and award the laurels to the team with the most points at the end.

SAUSAGES

Object of the game

To avoid laughing.

What you need

No special equipment needed.

How to play

Any game that requires players to refrain from laughing can be fiendishly difficult but here the difficulty is compounded by the requirement to answer any question put to you with the word "Sausages."

The game can be played in two ways, as a "hot seat" type game with one person at a time required to field questions fired at them by the rest of the group, or as an all-included game where anybody can ask anybody else a question at any time. In both cases the rule is the same, all questions must be answered with the reply "Sausages."

Good questions would be along the lines of "What do you keep in your pockets?" or "What do you find most attractive about your partners body?"

WHERE AM I?

Object of the game

To discover which country you have been sent to.

What you need

No special equipment needed.

How to play

Another game in which one guest has to suffer the ignominy of banishment from the room while everyone else tries to think up a conundrum, gets sidetracked and forgets all about them.

If you can keep your mind on the game for more than five minutes, it goes like this. The players in conference must decide on a country, or region or city to send the exile to. Working on scanty and obscure clues the exile has to figure out where he has been banished to.

Clues might be along the lines of "This country's flag is red and white," or "The head of state of this country comes from the oldest reigning dynasty in the world," or "This country is about half the size of France." Each player provides one tit-bit of information. The guesser can be given three chances to get it right, or points can be awarded depending on how many pieces of information it took before the answer was correctly deduced — five points for a correct answer after one clue, four points after two clues, three after three and so on.

WORD ASSOCIATIONS

Object of the game

To blurt out the first thing that comes into your head.

What you need

No special equipment needed.

How to play

Adapting psychiatrists' techniques for use as party games may not sound like a particularly entertaining idea, but this one at least can provide plenty of laughs.

Everybody knows the concept of word association – the analyst holds up an ink blot and the patient says the first thing that it reminds him of. In comedy sketches and pub jokes this usually results in the patient replying "Sex!" to every picture and the psychiatrist accusing them of being a sex maniac, to which the time-honoured reply is of course "Me, a sex manic? You're the one with all the dirty pictures!"

Ink blots are thankfully not required for this game, and sex maniacs are purely optional. With all players seated in a circle, one starts the ball rolling by saying a word. It can be any word at all, including the name of a person present. The player to his or her left must immediately say the first associated word that pops into their head. Continue around the circle, eliminating players that hesitate too long.

CALL MY BLUFF

Object of the game

To spot the correct definition of a word.

What you need

A dictionary and pens and paper for all players.

How to play

Familiar from years on our TV screens, Call My Bluff is a game easily adapted to a party setting as long as someone is prepared to put in some preparatory work beforehand. A popular variation of the game requires players to think up their own definitions, which requires more thought on the part of participants but has the advantage of being more competitive and involving.

In the classic, television-inspired, version the host selects a number of extremely obscure words from a weighty dictionary and thinks up two false definitions for each one. These are written on cards, along with the genuine definitions taken from the dictionary. In play, teams take it in turns to present their three definitions of the word in question while the opposing team attempts to figure out or, more usually, guess which one is correct.

A variant requires every player to compose their own definition of the announced mystery word. These are then collected and read out to the group by the host, who also includes the genuine dictionary definition. Players vote on which one they think is correct in each case, receiving two points for every vote cast for their own definition and one point for identifying the correct definition.

KEY WORDS

Object of the game

To think of a title containing the key word.

What you need

A pre-prepared list of words.

How to play

Prepare a list of words that often crop up in song, film or book titles. Examples could include "love," "happy," "never" and "time." When players are assembled, select a category and a word and go around the circle requiring everyone to supply a title in that category that includes that word.

BUZZ FIZZ

Object of the game

To replace certain numbers with the words "Buzz" and "Fizz."

What you need

No special equipment required.

How to play

This game should be played as rapidly as possible with hesitations of more than a second being punished with elimination. Players sit in a circle and begin to count in turn. The first player calls out "One," the second "Two," the third "Three" and so on. When the count gets to seven, or any multiple if seven, a player must say "Buzz" rather than the number. For numbers of more than one digit that contain a seven, "Buzz" replaces just the seven digit – so seventeen becomes "Buzzteen," twenty-seven "Twenty-buzz," and seventy-four "Buzzty four."

If this is proving too easy the Fizz rule should also be introduced. This requires the use of the word "Fizz" in the same relationship to the number five as "Buzz" is used in relationship to the number seven. Numbers that are multiples of both seven and five become "Buzz Fizz."

ENDLESS STORY

Object of the game

To keep a story going for as long as possible.

What you need

A stopwatch.

How to play

Players sit on the floor cross-legged in a circle as if around a campfire. If this brings back too many ghastly memories for some guests you can throw convention to the wind and allow players to sit wherever you like. Since this is what most of them will end up doing anyway, why fight it?

One player begins telling a story on any subject of their choosing and must continue for thirty seconds. At the end of that period, the next player must take over and continue the story in a logical way. Time must end on exactly thirty seconds, hence the stopwatch, which often results in stopping a speaker mid-sentence. The next player must continue the story from exactly the point it was left off. For example, if one storyteller gets as far as "Bob and Rose rounded the corner in their brand new . . ." the next player could continue with "four-wheel drive milk float laden with the hacked-off limbs of their morning's evil work."

Players who hesitate unduly or make the appalling mistake of ending the story are eliminated. The last player talking wins the game, and a license to practise as a wandering minstrel.

BALLOON ROLLERS

Object of the game

To hold a balloon in place without bursting it.

What you need

An inflated balloon for each pair of players.

How to play

Although it involves balloons, and is consequently rather silly, this game could hardly be described as frenetic by even the most athletically-challenged of party-goers. An excellent game for producing pseudo-erotic activity without the risk of faces being slapped or relationships shattered.

All guests are requested to pair-off and each couple is provided with a balloon. Standing face-to-face each couple position their balloon so that it is wedged securely between their bodies at about waist height.

On the word "Go!" both members of each team must attempt to turn three complete circles on the spot, without bursting or dropping their balloon. This requires a fair degree of co-operation since both team members must complete their three turns and end up facing one another at the end.

NOSE DETECTIVES

Object of the game

To identify substances by their smell alone.

What you need

A selection of substances with distinctive odours, bowls, thin cloths, pens and paper.

How to play

Place a sample of each of your smelly substances in each bowl and cover them with thin cloths. A good range of suitably scented items might include crushed garlic, white spirit, linseed oil, lavender, furniture polish, bleach, sage and tobacco.

Players take it in turns to walk along the line of covered dishes writing down what they think each one contains based on the information provided by hearty sniffing alone. The player with the most sensitive conk wins the day.

MATCH TOWER

Object of the game

To build a tower of matches.

What you need

An empty wine bottle and lots of matches.

How to play

Given that this game requires steady hands, it might be better if the wine bottle had been emptied on a previous occasion rather than by those attempting to play, but that's too much to ask.

Place two matches parallel to each other but separate across the open mouth of the wine bottle, and then place two more matches on top of them in the same configuration but at ninety degrees to the first two.

Players take it in turns to add one match at a time keeping to the same pattern. The object is to build the tower as high as possible, so any player whose actions result in its collapse should be required to perform a forfeit, such as running down to the shops to fetch another bottle of wine.

SHADOW PLAY

Object of the game

To identify objects by their shadows alone.

What you need

A large white sheet and a selection of fairly large household objects.

How to play

Said to be a Victorian parlour game favourite, this takes a little effort to set up but can be most amusing, particularly if played with the "mystery guest" variation.

Set up a white sheet in such a way that it hangs vertically to form a clearly visible screen. Position a lamp some distance behind the screen so that it is brightly and evenly illuminated. Players sit on the other side of the sheet and attempt to identify objects by their shadows as the host holds them up behind the sheet. Objects should be held at oblique angles so that their shadows are foreshortened or stretched in odd ways. Suitable objects might include an iron, a light bulb, a mobile phone, a corkscrew, a shoe and a comb.

A variation of this game allegedly enjoyed by Queen Victoria has guests themselves as the shadow casting objects using silly walks and props such as hats to disguise their silhouettes. For party-goers with slightly more risqué tastes the person behind the screen could be required to stand in a normal pose, but dressed only in their underwear.

CARAVAGGIO

Object of the game

To guess the identity of a famous person from just the initial letter of their name.

What you need

No special equipment needed.

How to play

A good alternative to regular guessing games because it requires as much skill on the part of the guessers as it does from the interrogated.

The game starts with one player settling on the name of a famous person — they can be dead or alive, real or fictitious — and announcing the initial letter of their last name to the other players. Participants then take it in turns to put questions in an attempt to discover the identity of the mystery celebrity.

Questions must, at least in the first stages, take the form of indirect guesses. For example, if it is announced that the name begins with letter "S," a valid question might be "Are you the author of Hamlet?" to which the answer should be "No, I am not William Shakespeare." Another question might be "Are you a former dictator of Soviet Russia?" to which the correct response would be "No, I am not Joseph Stalin."

The questioners' goal is to ask an indirect question that the player who thought of the celebrity name cannot answer. A player might ask "Are you the author of Billion Year Spree?" thinking of Brian Aldiss. If the other player is not a science fiction fan, he or she will have to admit that they cannot answer the question. In this situation the player who put the query is allowed a direct question along the lines of "Are you alive?" or "Are you fictional?" Only by generating enough of these direct-question opportunities will the secret celebrity (Homer Simpson in this case) be un-covered.

REVERSE ASSOCIATIONS

Object of the game

To recall a string of word associations.

What you need

No special equipment needed.

How to play

This game cunningly combines the delights of a word association game with the rigours of a memory recall game. Played by guests seated in a circle it begins with one participant announcing any word – "Curry" for example. For one circuit of the circle, the game proceeds as a normal word association round, with each player in turn saying the first thing that comes into their head.

When play returns to the guest who started the round, he or she must give the last word in the list of associations generated in the first round. Each successive player must give the next word from the list, always working in reverse order. Obviously the player who started the round has an easy task because all he has to do is repeat the word given by the player sitting next to him, namely the player who completed the list of associations. To keep things fair, the opportunity to start the next chain of word associations skip to the left at the beginning of each new round.

Players that hesitate too long, or that cannot remember the sequence are eliminated from the circle. The key to success in this game is to work out which player in the circle is your opposite number – the player who is the same number of spaces before the finish point as you are after it – and to pay special attention to whatever they say during the associations round.

MINOR ALTERATIONS

Object of the game

To spot minor changes.

What you need

Any normal room.

How to play

A compelling game that is very easy to play but which tests guests' attention to detail to the limit. Divide players into equal teams and choose one team to go first. Whichever team is selected should be given about a minute to study the room as thoroughly as they can, but don't tell them the kind of thing they should be looking for. At the end of a minute, usher them out of the room and lock the door.

Within a reasonable period of time the other team makes several subtle alterations to the contents of the room. Good options include swapping the positions of ornaments or pictures on the wall turning a rug around to face the opposite direction and, sneakiest of all, hiding some small objects completely out of sight.

Assuming the other team members haven't got bored and wandered off to find some other form of entertainment, invite them back in and set them the task of spotting the alterations. It's entirely up to you whether you tell them how many they are looking for or not, but they should expect there to be at least six or seven. The team that spots the largest number of the other team's changes wins the game.

WHAT'S MY TOWN

Object of the game

To discover the name of a mystery town.

What you need

An atlas might be handy.

How to play

One player is sent from the room while the others decide on the name of a well-known town or city somewhere in the world. Ideally, the chosen town should have the same number of letters as there are players, but this isn't essential if some players are willing to sit out or work in partnership with someone else.

Each player or pair is assigned one letter from the name of the town and has to come up with the name of another, completely un-connected city, that begins with the same letter. For example, if the secret city is Vienna, one player will need to think of a city that begins with "V" another with "I" another with "E" and so on.

When the absent player is wheeled back in he asks each player in succession to give him three clues about their town. So the player who had the letter "V" from Vienna, and thought of Venice as their town, can mention gondolas, canals and the Bridge of Sighs — these are rather easy clues, they can be much harder if you wish. With this information the guesser should be able to pinpoint Venice and ascertain that one of the letters that makes up the name of the secret city is "V."

Once the guesser has identified as many letters as he or she can from the clues, he attempts to identify the name of the secret city.

YES AND NO

Object of the game

To avoid using the words "Yes," and "No."

What you need

No special equipment needed.

How to play

A game that has put in an appearance on many a TV game show over the years, and is always worth throwing into the mix for a truly catholic party-going experience. In the classic version, one person acts as question master, but it's more fun if everybody is allowed to shout out questions as they think of them.

The point of the game is, of course, to avoid using the words "Yes" or "No" in response to any question. It sounds easy, but when the questions are coming thicker than snowflakes in a blizzard, and some of them are of a highly inflammatory nature, it's very easy to slip up.

Some people have an eerie talent for this game so, if a player hasn't succumbed after about five minutes, you should probably just give up and allow them to claim the title of undisputed champion.

QUEER QUESTIONS

Object of the game

To include two unlikely objects in the answer to a question.

What you need

A pre-prepared list of questions, pens and two slips of paper for all guests.

How to play

A piece of pure silliness, this game will be enjoyed by surrealists and Monty Python fans alike. Before guests arrive, prepare a set of extremely daft questions along the lines of "How do you keep your teeth so clean and bright?" or "Did you hurt yourself when you fell from heaven?"

To start play, give each player two slips of paper and ask them to write the name of an object on each one, the stranger and more impractical the object named the better. Examples might include the Eiffel Tower, a fishbone, chewed gum, a silicone breast implant and the Bishop of Bath and Wells' toupee.

Each player draws two slips of paper from a hat or similar container and has to come up with an answer to one of the host's question that makes mention of the two objects written on those slips. The player who comes up with the most convincing or amusing answer should be judged the winner.

WHY, WHEN, HOW AND WHERE

Object of the game

To guess a mystery object on the strength of replies to just four questions.

What you need

No special equipment needed.

How to play

Each player takes it in turns to be ejected from the room while the others think of a mystery object. The object can be just about anything, as long as it's fairly commonplace. Good examples might include a teapot, a bowling ball, a tumble drier or a diary.

Players are only allowed to ask four questions to help them guess the mystery object: "Why do you like it?" "When do you like it?"

"How do you like it?" and "Where do you like it?" The responses must be true, but designed to keep the mystery going as long as possible. A sequence of answers like "Because it helps me on dates," "On birthdays and bank holidays," "Full and fat," and "In my pocket so that I can feel it," might be reasonable responses to questions about your diary but could lead to entirely different guesses as to what is being described.

RING STRING

Object of the game

To guess the location of a ring.

What you need

A long piece of string and a ring.

How to play

Seat all players, except one, in a circle on the floor. Cut a piece of string long enough so that each player can hold on to it in his or her lap at the same time. Slip a ring onto the string and tie it into a loop so that the ring can be passed from player to player without ever leaving the string.

Players attempt to pass the ring to each other without being noticed by the watcher standing in the centre of the circle. The ring can be passed to the left or the right. At any point the watcher can accuse a player of being in possession of the ring and, if he or she is correct, watcher and player swap positions.

FINGER TRAP

Object of the game

To avoid getting your finger caught in the trap.

What you need

A long piece of string.

How to play

Choose a player to act as the trapper and seat everybody else in a circle. Players stretch out one arm so that all of their forefingers are upraised and more or less touching in the centre of the circle. The trapper places a noose made from a slip knot in the string around the collection of fingers and stands outside the circle holding the other end.

With the word "Snap!" the trapper pulls the string as swiftly as he can and players attempt to whip their fingers away before they are caught in the trap. Any player trapped in this way, or any player who skittishly pulls their finger away before the trapper says "Snap!" is eliminated from the circle.

Theoretically, the last player left in the circle wins the game, but it's unlikely that the trapper will be able to catch anyone once there are only two or three players left.

FORTUNATELY UNFORTUNATELY

Object of the game

To follow bad news with good and vice versa.

What you need

An even mix of pessimists and optimists.

How to play

Another venerable word game that has been played since before anybody knew what an optimist or a pessimist was. As with all great games, the rules are simple but can produce highly amusing results.

Players take it in turns to make a series of alternating statements that begin with the words "Fortunately," and "Unfortunately." Statements must follow on logically from the previous statement, but put a gloss or downer on the information as appropriate. An example might go something like this: "Fortunately, I remembered my wallet when I left this morning," "Unfortunately, there was nothing in it," "Fortunately, I found twenty pounds on the bus," "Unfortunately, it was in someone else's pocket," "Fortunately, they didn't notice the theft," "Unfortunately, the off-duty police officer sitting behind me did. . ."

Any player who is unable to continue the story without a long hesitation, or who gives the wrong kind of statement is eliminated or asked to perform a forfeit.

CONSEQUENCES

Object of the game

To create a story one word at a time.

What you need

Large sheets of paper and pens all round.

How to play

Another truly classic game that requires hardly any mental or physical effort except that necessary to laugh your socks off.

Each player receives a sheet of paper on which they write down the next element of the story without seeing the elements that have gone before. Once a line is filled in, the sheet is folded over so that the next player cannot see what was written, and it is passed on. At the same time as they pass one sheet to the left, players are receiving another from the right.

The lines of information build up to create a bizarre and un-expected story on each sheet of paper. In order for this to happen a sequence of rules must be followed. Before each sheet is passed around, a number sequence from one to thirteen should be written down the left hand side. Players fill in the numbered line at the top of each folded piece they are handed according to the following instructions:

1 An adjective describing a person's character or general appearance.
2 The name of a woman – real or fictitious.

3 The word "Met," followed by an adjective describing a person's character or general appearance.
4 The name of a man – real or fictitious.
5 The word "at," followed by a location – real or fictitious.
6 The words "They met" followed by the purpose or circumstances of their meeting.
7 The time at which they met.
8 The words "She said to him" followed by what she said to him.
9 The words "And he replied" followed by his reply.
10 What she did then.
11 What he did then.
12 The words "And consequently" followed by the consequence of their actions.
13 The words "And the moral of our story is" followed by a moral.

Results should come out something like this:

Shifty
Victoria Beckham
Met Vigorous
Homer Simpson
At Albert Square
They met to haggle
On Christmas Eve
She said to him "Are you lonesome tonight?"
And he replied "Love is like a butterfly."
Then she threw caution to the wind
Then he drew a line in the sand
And consequently they shared a cab home
And the moral of our story is, an apple never falls far from the tree.

HANGMAN

Object of the game

To guess a word before the gallows can be completed.

What you need

Large sheets of paper or a blackboard.

How to play

Whoever first thought of combining word-guessing with an in-strument of public execution must have been a very strange individual indeed, but he or she deserves our thanks for creating one of the most effortlessly absorbing games around.

Each player takes it in turns to be the hangman and thinks of a six or seven letter word which is represented by a dash for each letter chalked up in a line on the board. Other players take it in turns to guess letters (starting with vowels is a tried and tested tactic) and, if they get a letter right, the hangman must write that letter in its correct place or places above the dashes. If a guess is wrong, the hangman draws another element of the gallows. If the gallows and corpse are completed before the word is guessed, the successful hangman wins a point or gets to have another go.

One of the fundamental problems with Hangman as a game is that nobody can agree on how many elements to the gallows and body there should. Authorities tend to differ between eleven and thirteen, so make sure everyone knows which version you are playing. Here is an example of a thirteen element gallows – surely the most appropriate:

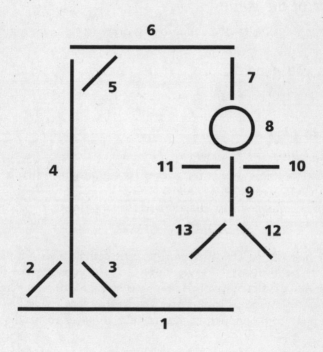

DRAWN CHARADES

Object of the game

To guess the subject of a scene being drawn by a team mate.

What you need

Large sheets of paper and pens or pencils.

How to play

Very much like Charades in that one team member has to get information across without speaking, but different in that drawing rather than miming is the form of communication. Teams will need to be equipped with blackboards or large sheets of paper set up on easels.

Before play begins the host will have to come up with a list of scenes to be illustrated. Movie, book, television or theatre titles can be used or, alternatively, scenes from real life or the imagination such as "Pavarotti in the park" or "Judgement day in Ealing." There need to be enough scenes for every player to have a go.

Divide guests into two equal teams and arrange them around their respective easels. One player from each team approaches the host and both are given the first scene on the list. Without uttering a word, both starters rush back to their teams and attempt to draw the scene or title that they have been given. Unlike ordinary Charades, the whole title or scene should be illustrated at once.

Once the first scene has been guessed by one team or the other, the next two team members are given the next scene on the list. The team that guesses the most scenes first claims victory.

CONSUMERS

Object of the game

To identify elements of advertisements.

What you need

Lots of advertisements cut from magazines and pens and paper all round.

How to play

A game that tests whether players are good little consumers or radical long-haired anti-capitalists at heart. It requires a fair amount of preparation, but the results can be surprising enough to make the effort worthwhile.

Cut out full-page ads from glossy magazines, Sunday supplements and other printed sources, for as many different products as you can find. Select a part of the image that doesn't include or make any written reference to the product being advertised and snip it out. Paste each of these excerpts onto cards and number each one.

To play, lay the cards out on a table so that the numbers are clearly visible, and give guests five to ten minutes to identify as many products as they can from these fragmented images. It's quite amazing how just a square of a particular colour can be instantly associated with certain products. Either people are a lot more observant than they are given credit for, or advertisers are just as deviously effective as has always been suspected.

THE BURNING HOUSE

Object of the game

To describe what you would rescue if your house was on fire.

What you need

Pen and paper all round.

How to play

A game that should have pyromaniacs salivating and everyone else consumed with mirth. To prepare, the host will need to write the names of ordinary, or not so ordinary, household objects on slips of paper. There should be five slips of paper per guest. Fold the slips twice and place them all into a hat or other container.

Hand each player a pre-prepared answer sheet that has the numbers one to five in a column on the left and the words "I would rescue my" followed by a space, followed by the word "because" and a larger space where a reason can be written. Guests are asked to fill in the reason for rescue, but NOT the item they are thinking of. For example, if a guest is thinking of rescuing his stamp collection, he should leave the space before the word "because" blank but write "I've had it since I was a child" in the space afterwards.

When all players have filled in all five of their reasons, the host shouts "Fire!" and guests dive into the hat containing the folded slips of paper and pull out five each. Unfolding their slips of paper one at a time, players fill in the objects they find written on each, working from number one on their lists down to number five.

Hopefully you should get results something like this:

I would rescue my WOODEN LEG because it belonged to my mother.

I would rescue my TOENAIL CLIPPERS because they were a wedding present.

I would rescue my IRONING BOARD because it reminds me of good times.

I would rescue my FRIDGE MAGNET because it's the most valuable thing I own.

I would rescue my PASSPORT because I made it with my own hands.

FAMOUS NAMES

Object of the game

To guess the names of famous people from descriptions.

What you need

Pen and paper.

How to play

Prepare lots of slips of paper, each one bearing the name of a famous person or fictitious character. Fold all the slips and place them in the ubiquitous hat.

Divide players into small teams of three or four and give the hat to the team that has elected to go first. One team member pulls a slip from the hat, reads the name written on it, and then attempts to convey this information to his or her team mates using mime or verbal description. At no point must he or she say either the forename or surname written on the card, or use "sounds like" to help their team mates.

Players who break the rules end their team's turn. When a name is guessed correctly, the team should retain that slip; if they decide to give up on one and try another, the slip goes back in the hat. Play continues from team to team until all the slips have been won. The team with the most slips at the end wins the game.

NOISES OFF

Object of the game

To identify noises.

What you need

A recording device and pens and paper all round.

How to play

This is a game that requires a lot of preparation on the part of the host, but the up-side is that the preparation can be as much fun as actually playing.

Use a tape recorder, or any other audio recording device, to capture a range of odd and unusual noises. These could include uncorking a bottle of wine, chewing a biscuit, using a toilet brush, clipping your toenails, baked beans popping in a microwave oven or, if you are a particularly adventurous type, the call of the Yeti on a windblown Himalayan night. Ensure that each sound in your sequence is separated by a few seconds of silence.

Players are equipped with pens and paper and have the task of writing down what they think each noise is as they hear it. Play the sequence once, give a few minutes for thought, then play it a second and final time. Stand firm against demands that it be played a third time. When answers are checked points should be given for accuracy. The player who guesses that a sound was made by something popping in a microwave should get less points than the sharp-eared individual who guessed that it was baked beans.

WHERE IN THE WORLD

Object of the game

To identify countries from their shapes.

What you need

An atlas.

How to play

To prepare for this game you need to trace the outlines of a fifteen or twenty countries from an atlas, preferably one that's fairly up to date. Your tracings can be scaled-down to fit on two or three sheets of paper using a photocopier or each presented on a separate sheet. Either way, each country outline should be numbered.

Players have five or ten minutes to identify as many countries as possible, writing their answers on separate pieces of paper. You'll find that island nations, or nations with long coastlines, such as Ireland or Canada are the easiest to identify, so include lots of landlocked countries too, particularly African ones with their strangely artificial straight-line borders.

TRICK MEMORY TRAY

Object of the game

To remember items on a tray.

What you need

A tray, a cloth and various small items.

How to play

The Memory Tray is a classic party favourite that can be spiced-up with a couple of simple variations. In the basic game, players are allowed to examine a tray holding about ten to twelve objects for thirty seconds, before it is covered with a cloth and removed. When the tray returns, one item will have been removed, and players have to identify what is missing.

A simple variation that practically everyone must have come across should be introduced after a few rounds. Instead of removing an object from the tray, replace it with a similar object and see if anyone notices.

A few rounds later you can play the following trick. Display the tray as usual for thirty seconds, then take it away. Rather than removing an object, however, the person bearing the tray should alter some subtle aspect of their appearance. Examples could include, changing earrings, putting a ring on a different finger, putting glasses on or taking them off, changing shoes, or removing a belt. Players, who have been focusing all their attention on the tray, are now asked to identify the change in the tray-bearer's appearance.

CASTAWAYS

Object of the game

To identify a famous person by his or her survival gear.

What you need

Pens and paper all round.

How to play

A variation on the classic "What would you take to a desert island" scenario. Prepare a list of famous people, real or fictitious, and write the names on slips of paper to be drawn from a hat. Divide players into two teams and allow each player to draw one name from the hat.

Players have five or ten minutes to think up a list of five items that their celebrity would probably want to take to a desert island. Team mates will be required to guess the identity of the famous person on the basis of these items, so they should be as revealing as possible. Clearly, Popeye wouldn't want to go anywhere without a pipe, a sailor suit, a tin opener, some cans of spinach and a little Olive Oil. Others aren't so easy to characterize.

The game can also be played with each participant listing what they think another guest would want with them in the event of a shipwreck, although this only really works when players know each other pretty well.

IN GOOD VOICE

Even if your musical abilities are restricted to tuneless warbling in the shower there's plenty of fun to be had with the games in this short but harmonically composed section. Most of these games involve dancing, or at least staggering, along to music so if the word karaoke brings you out in a cold sweat you should have nothing to fear.

MUSICAL SQUADS

Object of the game

To form into groups when the music stops.

What you need

Music.

How to play

A variation of Musical Statues that requires players to form themselves into groups with appropriate number of members when the music stops.

With everybody prancing happily around the room to the music, the host suddenly shuts it off and shouts "Threes!" or "Fours!" or "Sixes!" or "Sevens!" Players must immediately attempt to form a group of that size with anyone close enough to grab.

For a group to be considered properly formed its members must be in a ring with their arms tightly clasped around each others' shoulders. Anyone not able to insinuate themselves into a group is eliminated. Hosts who wish to bring a premature halt to the proceedings when there are still three of four players left on the dance floor should simply shout "Sixteens."

MUSICAL STATUES

Object of the game

To remain absolutely still when the music stops,

What you need

A good selection of tunes.

How to play

A favourite at children's parties, this energetic game works equally well with adults, especially those profoundly deficient in the rhythm and agility departments.

As everybody knows, when the music stops, you stop. This can be easier said then done if you are in the midst of a vaulting leap that would put Travolta to shame. A good host will wait until players are in mid-air or halfway through a spectacular gyration before cutting off the music. Rejoice as bodies rain down in the ensuing silence.

MUSICAL TICKLERS

Object of the game

To remain still when the music stops despite assaults with a feather duster.

What you need

Music and a few feather dusters.

How to play

Played exactly as Musical Statues but with the important addition of a feather duster-wielding host. Players who fail to freeze quickly enough when the music stops are still eliminated, but those that remain must continue to remain motionless even when provoked by the application of a feather duster.

To enhance the challenge even further, eliminated players should be armed with their own tickling sticks and allowed to join in the torment in the next round. For the ultimate in Carry On type naughtiness, the game should be played with dancers clad in tank tops so that they can be really tickled.

MARCHING ORDERS

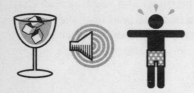

Object of the game

To carry out the orders of the sergeant major.

What you need

Martial music and two chairs.

How to play

A compilation of marching band tunes is ideal for this game, but it could equally be played with lilting Celtic ballads to good ironic effect. Place two chairs at opposite ends of the room before assembling the troops.

As long as the music is playing, guests march up and down the length of the room, around the two chairs, arms swinging, shoulders back and chests very much to the fore. As soon as the music stops, they must perform a drill described by the sergeant major.

The drill could be anything from the innocent hopping-on-one-leg-while-saluting manoeuvre, to the outrageous underwear inspection which requires trousers to be dropped and skirts to be raised. Soldiers failing to perform the correct drill are escorted to the guard house under armed guard.

RANDOM RHYTHM

Object of the game

To avoid being caught with the rhythm stick in your hand.

What you need

Music and a long stick or cane.

How to play

Players stand in a circle and the host stands with his or her back to them in control of the music system. One player is armed with a stick or cane which should be long enough that its end can be banged on the floor from a standing position.

As long as the music is playing competitors must knock the end of the stick on the floor three times before passing it to the player on his or her left. Any player caught still holding the stick when the music stops is eliminated until only the winner remains.

In theory, the stick should hit the floor in some kind of rhythm with the music. In practice, players are so keen to get rid of the thing that they tend to tap away as fast as possible. As long as each player produces three distinct taps before passing the stick on it shouldn't matter.

MUSICAL HATS

Object of the game

To be wearing a hat when the music stops.

What you need

A selection of hats – one less than there are players.

How to play

A musical game that places the emphasis on the head rather than the buttocks may seem slightly more cerebral than its cousins, that is until you see grown men tussling for possession of the last floral bonnet. Hats to be used in the game should be as varied as possible and as cheap as possible given the conditions they are likely to encounter.

Players sit in a circle with the hats circulating as long as the music plays. Hat-passing is achieved by removing the hat from your own head with the right hand and placing it on the head of the player to the right in one fluid movement. When everyone does this at the same time the result is quite as spectacular and satisfying as the game itself.

When the music ceases players may go to any lengths to grab or retain a hat for their own head, as long as they don't leave their chairs or bring offensive weapons into play. Any player left hatless exits the circle taking his or her chair, and a hat from the stockpile, with them. Theoretically, the game should continue until there is just one player left, but the bloodshed involved in getting to that point may be too much to bear.

MUSICAL ISLANDS

Object of the game

To find dry land when the music stops.

What you need

Music and several pieces of card.

How to play

A rollicking combination of Musical Statues and Musical Chairs, this game has contestants struggling to find a foothold on an ever-diminishing archipelago of islands. To play, you will need several pieces of stout card which should be scattered around the playing area. Bear in mind that people will be leaping onto these cards, so make sure they're not going to slip too easily.

While the music is playing everyone prances merrily around the room – Beach Boys hits or something with a tropical island feel would fit the musical bill perfectly. As soon as the music stops, however, everyone must make for the nearest island.

More than one person may stand on an island, but both feet must be completely clear of the floor and they must be able to hold position for five seconds without toppling into the sea. Players that fail to comply are of course eliminated. Remove one island after every stoppage and keep going until only one player is left.

MAESTRO

Object of the game

To sing a song while disguising your voice.

What you need

A pencil or some other substitute for a conductor's baton.

How to play

One player is selected to be the Maestro and stands, blindfolded and equipped with a baton, in the centre of a circle formed by the other players. Each player must select a well-known tune or song and hum it loudly as the ring circulates around the blind Maestro.

As long as the Maestro is merrily waving his or her baton, the players continue to circulate but, as soon as the baton stops, they too must freeze where they are and remain absolutely silent. Using the baton, the Maestro points in any direction, and the player indicated has to sing his or her song out loud using a silly or disguised voice. If the Maestro is able to guess who is singing the song, that player is eliminated from the circle or, alternatively, takes the place of the Maestro.

CONDUCTOR

Object of the game

To imitate the sounds of various musical instruments.

What you need

No special equipment needed.

How to play

Choose one person to be the Conductor and form everyone else into a circle around him. At any moment the Conductor can point to a player and require them to make the sound of the desired instrument, with accompanying mimed action where appropriate. Any player deemed by the Conductor to be hopelessly inaccurate in his or her imitation of the requested instrument is ejected from the circle.

This game can also be played with the Conductor blindfolded and the other players circling around until one or other of them is selected by a pointed finger. This lessens the likelihood of unfair victimisation by the Conductor, but then where's the fun in that?

MIND THE HOLE

Object of the game

To avoid being pulled into the hole.

What you need

A hoola-hoop or some coloured sticky tape.

How to play

Be warned, this is an extremely physical game in which tugging, pushing, and tripping other players are all acceptable moves. Do not play this game unless you are prepared to accept the consequences.

Place the hoop on the floor, or use tape to form a circle of a similar size. All players form a circle around the hoop and link arms. When the music starts, the jolly gang dance in a circle around the gaping hole that the hoop represents, their arms remaining linked at all times. All players have to avoid doing is placing a foot inside the circle. This is a lot more easily said than done, however, when everyone else is allowed to push, pull or barge you in any way they see fit.

Placing a foot within the circle is the equivalent of plunging into a bottomless pit but has the beneficial side effect of elimination from the game and an opportunity for a nice lie down in a darkened room. Keep playing until only one player remains outside the pit or until people are no longer able to stand.

THEME TUNES

Object of the game

To guess the theme tune.

What you need

No special equipment needed.

How to play

Assemble a list of television programmes with recognizable and well-known theme tunes (soap operas are a good bet) and write each one on a slip of paper. These slips should be folded and placed in a receptacle of some kind.

Divide players into couples or teams of three before play begins. For each round, one member of each team draws a slip of paper and attempts to hum, whistle or otherwise convey it by sound to his or her team mates. Hand clapping, thigh slapping and all manner of vocalizations are allowed, but players must not actually sing or speak words. If guessed correctly, the team retains the slip of paper and the next team has a go. Total up slips of paper at the end to ascertain the winners.

This game can of course be played with songs or even movie theme tunes if you feel your guests would be up to it.

LIFE AND SOUL

This is where the classics live – the games that have proven themselves to be winners over countless hours of party-time. Who needs high-tech and virtual reality when the real world can provide such timeless entertainment as a round of Blind Man's Buff or Murder in the Dark? A quick read through this section and you will be chomping at the bit to get the next party organized as soon as possible.

PSYCHIC

Object of the game

To discover the psychic trick.

What you need

No special props are required.

How to play

The entire game rests on a simple code. Before the game is even announced the Psychic and the Assistant must secretly agree on a code. The easiest is the "white before" code. This means that the Psychic will always point to a white object immediately before he or she points to the chosen object. The Assistant knows that whenever the Psychic points to a white object, the next thing he or she points to will be the chosen object. There are many obvious variations on this code. You could use "black before" or "white, black before" codes for example. Bear in mind that the more complicated your code the more difficult it will be for players to spot it and the more likely you are to make mistakes, so it's best to stick to a simple one.

All players must be in the same room. The Psychic announces that he or she is able to communicate telepathically with his or her Assistant and can prove it. The Assistant leaves the room and all other players silently agree on any object in the room, they then indicate the chosen object to the Psychic. Let's assume that the players choose a television for this example.

The Assistant is called back into the room. The Psychic points to any object in the room that isn't white and isn't the chosen object, and asks the Assistant "Is this it"? It's best if the Psychic goes right up to an object and physically touches it with a finger. The Assistant answers "No." The Psychic continues to point at objects in the room, none of them white, and asks the question "Is this it?" After five or six objects, the Psychic points to a white object, a light switch for example, and asks "Is this it?" The Assistant answers "No", but he or she now knows that the next object the Psychic points to will be the one chosen by the players. Finally the Psychic points to chosen object, the television, and asks "Is this it?" The Assistant can now confidently answer "Yes it is!"

Example of Play

Players: Quietly agree on an object in the room, the television, and point it out to the Psychic.

Psychic: "My assistant may enter the room now." Assistant enters and stands in the centre of the room.

Psychic: Goes up to a picture hanging on the wall and touches the silver frame with an index finger "Is this it?"

Assistant: "No."

Psychic: Crosses to wooden coffee table and pats it with a hand "Is it this?"

Assistant: "No."

Psychic: Turns and touches a red lampshade with two fingers "Is it this?"

Assistant: "No."

Psychic: Crosses room again and points to white light switch "Is it this?"

Assistant: "No"

Psychic: Walks to television and touches it with left hand "Is it this?"

Assistant: "Yes, that's it!"

The Assistant leaves the room again and the players choose another object which the Psychic is able to communicate using the "white before" code. This continues until a player thinks they know how the trick is done. The player must not shout out the solution, instead he or she must take the Assistant's place. The Psychic must act fairly and use exactly the same "white before" code with his or her new Assistant. If the player has guessed the trick correctly they will be able to identify the chosen object. The game continues until all players have guessed the code.

The role of the Psychic is very important in this game. To make things more interesting the Psychic should vary his or her behaviour while questioning the Assistant. For example, use the question "Is it this?" instead of "Is this it?" sometimes, or point to different objects using a different finger or the opposite hand. Once the players realise they are looking for some kind of code they will pick up on these variations. A player might guess that the chosen object is always pointed to with the left hand for example. The more cunning the Psychic is with his or her variations, the more challenging the game.

BLIND MAN'S BLUFF

Object of the game

To identify other players by voice alone.

What you need

A blindfold and a fairly large room.

How to play

Played at least since the time of the ancient Greeks the game known today as Blind Man's Bluff is a perennial party favourite. Choose somebody to go first and blindfold them – he or she becomes the "Blind Man". The Blind Man stands in the centre of the room and everybody else stands in various positions of their own choosing around the room. The Blind Man is spun around three times (gently!), so that he or she loses orientation. With arms outstretched the Blind Man stumbles around the room until he or she touches one of the other players. The other players are not allowed to move from where they have chosen to stand, but they can duck and lean to avoid being touched.

Once contact is made, the Blind Man has to try and identify the person he or she has touched. Exactly how the identification is made depends on the variation you decide to play. In the classic game identification is by touch, aided by any squeaks, laughs or gasps that the touched player cannot avoid making. If the Blind Man guesses the identity of the player correctly, then that player becomes the next Blind Man.

When the Victorians played this game the Blind Man had a long stick and had to identify those he touched by asking them three questions. A hundred years earlier nobles played the game as a good excuse to get their hands on the young ladies of the court. Every era has rules according to its accepted social conventions. There are almost endless possible variations, here are a few:

1 The Blind Man asks "Who are you?" and the touched player answers using a silly or disguised voice.

2 The players circulate around the room talking or singing loudly in disguised voices while the Blind Man stands still in the middle. At a given signal the players freeze where they are and the Blind Man is free to go towards somebody he or she recognizes.

3 When the Blind Man touches a player he or she makes a noise, snorts like a pig for example, and the player must make the same noise while trying to disguise his or her voice as much as possible.

4 If there are a lot of people available the players can form a ring around the Blind Man. The players circle around until the Blind Man claps three times, the Blind Man then points in any direction and the player chosen goes into the circle with the Blind Man. The chosen player must avoid being touched by the Blind Man, but cannot leave the circle. Once he or she is touched identification is by whatever method has previously been decided on.

5 In one, slightly more complex, version of the game the Blind Man is not actually blindfolded but has to identify players by their shadows. The Blind Man sits in a chair facing a blank wall with a single strong light behind him. The players walk behind the Blind Man, but in front of the lamp, so that their shadow is thrown onto the wall. Players may use silly walks or any available props to disguise their identity.

COCKTAIL PARTY

Object of the game

To identify the mystery guests.

What you need

No special props are required, but you will need a pair of blabbermouths who aren't afraid to make fools of themselves to get the ball rolling.

How to play

Two willing volunteers leave the room and agree who they are going to pretend to be. The idea is for them to conduct a conversation, so it helps if the chosen characters have something in common, but apart from that they can choose any two famous people, living or dead, fictional or real.

The two volunteers re-enter the room and talk to each other in the personas of their chosen characters. They should use phrases and mannerisms typical to their character but at the same time try to conceal their identities. The other players should be aware that there is a game going on, but the idea is not for them to sit around in a circle and listen intently, the conversation should blend into the general conversation in the room. The other players have to guess who the two volunteers are pretending to be and then join in the conversation in such a way that it is obvious to the actors that he or she has guessed.

The conversation continues until everyone has guessed the identity of the actors. As more and more people guess it becomes increasingly interesting, and infuriating for those who are still in the dark. There is plenty of scope for other players to give them hints and clues in the context of the conversation. An intriguing variation is to have other players take on their own secret identity to join in the conversation. This makes it more interesting for the two original actors since they now have the challenge of identifying the newcomer.

MURDERER!

Object of the game

To identify the winking murderer before you become a victim.

What you need

Practically any board game or card game will do.

Object of the game

Players have to identify the murderer in their midst before they become victims.

How to play

An almost unique game in that it is best played at the same time as another game – traditional board games such as Monopoly are ideal.

Take the same number of playing cards as players and put them into a box or other container; one of the cards must be a joker. If you haven't got playing cards, use folded pieces of paper and mark one with an "X." Each player draws one card, taking care not to let anyone see it, and checks to see if it's a joker (or an "X"). Once everybody has drawn a card, replace them all in the container and shake it up so that it's impossible for anyone to discover who got the joker.

The player who drew the joker is the Murderer and everybody else is a potential victim. The Murderer "kills" by winking at his or her victims. Anybody who is winked at waits ten seconds and then "dies" in a suitably theatrical and blood-curdling manner. Players have to figure out who the Murderer is before they get winked at, the Murderer has to keep his or her winking as subtle as possible to avoid detection. If a player thinks they know who the murderer is, but guesses wrong, they too are dead.

The advantages of playing this game at the same time as another game are obvious. With people's attention focused on another activity a devious winker can avoid detections for a long time. Without some kind of distraction the game tends to be over very quickly. Victims can of course continue with whatever other game is being played, they are just out of that round of Murderer.

Once the Murderer is discovered, the cards are redrawn and another round can get under way. The winner can be regarded as the Murderer who achieved the most victims before discovery, if anybody can be bothered to keep a score.

SITUATIONS

Object of the game

To guess what situation is being portrayed by other players.

What you need

Nothing more than imagination.

How to play

An extremely simple game that requires no preparation but which can be very entertaining.

One person is chosen to leave the room and removes themselves to a location where they can't hear what's going on. All the other players decide on a situation and arrange themselves into a frozen snapshot. For example, the situation could be an operating theatre, so one player could lie on a coffee table while all the others gather around posing as surgeons and nurses.

Once the scene is set up the exiled player is allowed back into the room and must decide what the situation is. The guesser is allowed to ask actors in the scene "yes" or "no" questions only.

Situations can be as mundane or bizarre as you want to make them. They can be from everyday life, or they could be scenes from famous movies or plays. Here's a list of suggestions:

Everybody is dying of the Black Death.
Waiting for a bus.
Dying of the Black Death while waiting for a bus.

Watching the 1966 World Cup final.
Macbeth meeting the three witches.
A funeral.
A murder trial.

MURDER IN THE DARK

Object of the game

To get away with murder.

What you need

Slips of paper and a container to draw them from.

How to play

A giant among classic party games, Murder in the Dark is a chilling experience even for the most strong-hearted of participants. This game has everything, tension, intrigue, theatrical screaming and ample groping opportunities. Best played in a large, spooky house on a storm-racked night, it can nevertheless be enjoyed in a two-roomed flat on a slightly damp evening in June.

The set-up is simplicity itself. Make identical slips of paper, one for each player, and write "Murderer" on one and "Detective" on another – leave all the other slips blank. Papers should be folded and placed in a container to allow each player to select one. Whoever draws the "Detective" slip must announce his identity to the other players; the murderer keeps understandably quiet.

Players scatter themselves around the house and all lights are turned off. Everybody wanders about, cracking shins on furniture and stumbling into unnoticed cupboards until the murderer strikes. A "kill" is performed by simply grasping a victim and whispering "You're dead!" in their ear, at which point the victim should scream in the most blood-curdling manner they can muster and fall lifeless to the floor.

When the scream is heard, everybody except the detective and murderer must freeze exactly where they are. The detective rushes to the scene, turning on lights as he goes, and the murderer can run, or freeze where he is and act like an innocent bystander. By questioning players the detective must try and unmask the murderer. Players must answer questions truthfully, but the murderer can lie as much as he likes. The detective has two chances to identify the killer; if asked directly "Are you the murderer?" the game is up and he or she must answer truthfully.

WINKERS

Object of the game

To attract players to empty chairs by winking.

What you need

Half as many chairs as players.

How to play

An excellent icebreaker as well as being a thoroughly decent, meaty game for the heart of a party. For its full risqué elements to emerge, it's highly desirable to have an almost equal number of men and women playing.

Arrange the chairs in a wide circle facing inwards. The women should occupy all but one of the chairs and one man should stand behind each woman with his hands resting on the back of her chair. There also needs to be a man standing behind the empty chair, the "bachelor" and what he does with his hands is entirely up to him.

Play begins with the bachelor. He must wink at one of the women and she, unable to resist his overwhelming charm, must rush across the circle to occupy his empty chair. The snag is that if the protective male standing behind her chair manages to place his hands on her shoulders before she can get away, the woman must remain where she is.

If the bachelor's winking ruse is unsuccessful on the first attempt, he must keep trying until he manages to lure another woman from the clutches of her jealous protector. Any man not paying sufficient attention to keep his woman seated becomes the next bachelor and must try to lure a replacement.

Before fist fights break out, it's a good idea to let the women have a go at winking and allow the men to cool-off with a bit of pointless running around. There is no real winner but the secret attractions revealed by overly-hasty attempts to break away from, or form up with, certain partners provide ample entertainment.

HANDS UP!

Object of the game

To guess the location of a coin held by the opposing team.

What you need

A coin and a table that everyone can sit around.

How to play

A fun and frantic game of observation and deduction with the added attraction that players get to bang on the table with gusto and extract cash from opponents. A table large enough to seat all players is a vital ingredient in this game since it provides cover for passing manoeuvres.

Divide guests into two equal teams and have the teams seated facing each other across the table. One group is chosen to go first – possibly on the result of a coin toss. Members of the team opening play pass the coin from person to person under the table until the captain of the opposing team shouts "Hands up!" at which point they must immediately raise their arms in the air with fists clenched, one of the fists concealing the coin. When the leader of the opposing team shouts "Hands down!" they must slam them down on the table with palms flat.

The opposing team now has to guess which hand is concealing the coin, assuming it hasn't already been flung across the table by a clumsy hands-down manoeuvre. If they guess correctly, the coin passes to them and it's the other team's turn to guess. Close observation is a vital element to this game, as is feigned passing and double-blind plays of all kinds. The biggest clue to locating the coin is the sound it makes hitting the table, defending teams should make their hands-down manoeuvre with a loud covering slap!

STACKS

Object of the game

To get four people on a chair without causing serious injury.

What you need

A pack of playing cards and some chairs.

How to play

Stuffed shirts can be lured into playing this game in the belief that it involves nothing more hazardous than a hand of cards, only to find themselves engaged in a riotous romp that any despotic emperor would have been proud of. The version described here requires that the total number of participating players be divisible by four, but it could fairly obviously be adapted to work for numbers divisible by three.

Produce the pack of playing cards and extract the ace, king, queen, and jack of each suit. Depending on how many players you have, select two, three or all four of the suits and shuffle the eight, twelve or sixteen cards together thoroughly. Lay the cards face down on the floor, and everything is set for action.

At the word "Go!" all players must rush forward and grab a card at random. As quickly as possible they must locate other players who hold cards of the same suit and get to the nearest empty chair. The player holding the ace sits down first, the king sits on his lap, the queen on his lap and the jack on top of the pile. The first players to form this precarious arrangement and hold it for five seconds win the game.

BLACK HATS AND WHITE HATS

Object of the game

To prevent the mean black hats from bursting your balloon.

What you need

A balloon and a selection of black hats and white hats.

How to play

Drawing on the western movie convention that the good guys wear white hats while the bad guys wear black, this game pitches the forces of darkness and light into a life and death struggle over the fate of a single, vulnerable balloon. For its full effect, black hats should be provided for the baddies and white ones for the goodies, although you could also use appropriately coloured cloths tied bandana-like around the forehead as a nod to Kurosawa.

As with all great dramas, the plot is simple. The white hats have an inflated balloon that they must fight to keep airborne, while black hats want nothing more than to bring it down to earth and grind its beneath their heels. It's all a touching metaphor for the struggle of the soaring human spirit against the forces of repression and degradation or, alternatively, its just another silly and violent thing you can do with a balloon.

When the forces of evil triumph, as they always seem to in the end, the teams can swap identities and explore the darker, or lighter, sides to their natures. Weapons of any kind are strictly forbidden, as is physically tackling opponents.

IN THE FRAME

Object of the game

To avoid laughing.

What you need

An empty picture frame large enough for a player to put their head through.

How to play

Another game that requires contestants to keep a straight face under almost unbearable psychological pressure. Very few people can complete this challenge successfully.

Each player in turn stands up and holds the picture frame so that it frames their head and shoulders. This pose must be held for two minutes (with eyes open) while everyone else does their level best to make the framed one crack a smile. Usually, simply peering at the victim is more than sufficient to cause them to collapse from nervous tension within a few seconds.

BLIND DRAWING

Object of the game

To draw accurately while blindfolded.

What you need

A blindfold, a blackboard and chalks, or a pad of A1 sized paper set up on an easel and some pens.

How to play

More of an excuse for outright hilarity than a game this challenge is equally as suited to born draughtsmen as art class dunces. If you can possible arrange a blackboard (a small kid's one will do), or some other large-scale surface to draw on, the results will be far more impressive.

Each guest takes it in turns to don the blindfold, take up the chalk and approach the blackboard (not necessarily in that order, unless you are going for a slapstick effect). Agree on an object to form the initial stage of the drawing, such as a house, or the figure of a man. Once the player has quickly sketched this to the best of his or her abilities other guests get to call out refinements to the scene that he or she must try and add.

For example, once the blindfolded player has drawn his house, a guest can call for the addition of a cat sitting on the lawn, or smoke billowing from the windows, or whatever else takes their fancy. Obviously, if the initial drawing is of the figure of a man the suggestions may be significantly funnier.

PARCEL DILEMMA

Object of the game

To pass the parcel without causing offence.

What you need

Brown paper, sticky tape and a small prize.

This is a game that combines all the innocent childhood pleasures of pass the parcel with the not so innocent adult pleasures of flirting with the opposite sex. An ideal exercise for groups of singles or, if you're in the mood to stir up trouble, for groups of established couples.

The game proceeds exactly as you will remember pass the parcel from childhood parties with the important proviso that the method of passing depends on personal preferences rather than the traditional stopping and starting of a dodgy vinyl LP.

On each layer of wrapping the host will have written an instruction along the lines of "Pass the parcel to the man with the nicest eyes," or "Pass the parcel to the woman with the shapeliest hips." Hosts can of course include instructions for the parcel to be passed to whoever the player regards as having the ugliest nose, or the meanest-looking mouth.

When the prize in the core of the parcel is finally unveiled it can be as insignificant or provocative as you choose, most people will be too busy fuming or swooning to notice.

HOW WOULD YOU LIKE IT?

Object of the game

To cause acute embarrassment.

What you need

Pen and paper for all guests.

How to play

Less of a game and more of a sneaky trick, this little exercise is a perfect example of the maxim do unto others as you would have them do unto you.

Prepare cards, each one bearing the name of a guest, and divide them into two piles; one for the men and the other for the women. When guests arrive, have the women take a card from the men's pile and vice versa. Ask everyone to write a challenge on the card they have chosen. It can be anything from standing on one leg for two minutes to stripping down to your underwear and making three circuits of the garden while singing the Birdie Song. Subtly encourage players to be as vindictive as possible.

When all cards are filled in and guests are simultaneously quaking at what they will be asked to do and anticipating other people's embarrassments, announce the unexpected twist to the game. Everyone assumes that the challenge will have to be performed by the guest whose name is on the card, in fact it's the person who wrote the challenge that has to perform it.

Sit back and enjoy the torment as the sadistic reap their just desserts and the meek inherit the Earth.

THE SHUFFLE

Object of the game

To pass a large fruit along a line of team members.

What you need

A grapefruit, melon, pumpkin or other large fruit for each team.

How to play

Divide players into two equal teams and sit them down on the floor in two rows facing each other. All players should have their legs stretched out in front of them with their heels together. Place the grapefruit on the ankles of the first player in each line.

Without touching the fruit with any other part of their bodies, players must roll the grapefruit from the shins of the first to the last team member in the line. If the grapefruit touches the floor or rolls away out of control at any point, the offending team must start again. For a slightly more tricky challenge an orange, or even an egg, could be used instead of the grapefruit.

GRANDPA'S FOOTSTEPS

Object of the game

To avoid being caught moving.

What you need

No equipment needed.

How to play

A classic kids' game that will provide far more entertainment than the most subtle of word games. It has the added advantage of extremely simple rules that not even the merriest of guests can forget – which isn't to say that the same state of merriment won't be a considerable handicap in sticking to them.

One player is chosen to be Grandpa and may be equipped with slippers, pipe and cap, if such items are readily available. It's Grandpa's job to stomp irritably around the room while everybody else follows in a crocodile behind him imitating his walk.

At any moment, and without warning, Grandpa may stop and spin round to catch his tormentors. Any player that he spots still moving is eliminated. The stomping continues until all but one player is out.

LAST STRAW

Object of the game

To pass a thimble between players using only a straw held in the mouth.

What you need

A straw for every player and a thimble for each team.

How to play

Another passing game that requires steady nerves. The game works best with teams restricted to about four or five members, otherwise it can go on forever. Each player is equipped with a drinking straw, which is held in the mouth and each team gets a thimble, which must be passed from the end of one player's straw to the next in line. You will probably need to experiment a bit with the drinking straws and thimbles to get a workable combination – it's no good if the thimble is so heavy that it simply causes the straws to buckle.

Players may be seated or standing, depending on your preference, but they must not touch their thimble with anything other than their straws and straws must remain firmly clamped, cigar-like, in players' mouths. Even thimbles that end up on the floor must be retrieved with straws alone. It's probably a good idea to exclude allergy sufferers from this game since sneezing during thimble-passing manoeuvres tends to be disastrous.

PASS IT ON

Object of the game

To squeeze other players' hands without being spotted.

What you need

Players with warm hands.

How to play

A very simple game that provides lots of opportunities for holding hands with members of the opposite sex. Choose one player to be the outcast and stand everybody else in a circle. The loner stands in the centre of the circle and surveys the other players with an eagle eye. One of the players in the circle must be chosen to start without the player in the centre knowing who it is.

The starting player must squeeze the hand of the player to the left or right of him in the circle, but he must do this without being spotted by the player in the centre. Whoever's hand is squeezed must pass the squeeze on to the next in line, also without being seen. Again, the squeeze can be passed to the left or the right. Any player who is spotted in the act takes his or her lonely place in the centre.

It's entirely up to you how you arrange guests in the circle. Boy-girl-boy-girl is, of course, traditional, but other arrangements might be more amusing. The greatest fun is to be had after attention starts to wander and there are shrieks of surprise as people suddenly find their hands grasped at totally unexpected moments.

BURBLE

Object of the game

To guess a secret verb.

What you need

No equipment needed.

How to play

Choose one player to exit the room and gather the others together in conference. With the outcast safely out of earshot, decide on a verb such as walk, dance, stroke or hobble. The verb can be as lewd or lavatorial as you like, but it's best to stick to things performed directly with the body. Retrieve the exiled player from his position with ear pinned to the keyhole and play is ready to begin.

The player who doesn't know what verb has been chosen has to try and figure it out by asking questions using the word "Burble" instead of the verb trying to be guessed. So a question might be "Do I burble with my hands?" If the mystery verb is "kick" for example, the answer would be a resounding "No!" Questions should only be answered "Yes" or "No" but, in reality, you'll probably have to allow "Sometimes" or "Maybe" as well.

Questions can be restricted to twenty, or the game can continue until the word is discovered or the guesser gives up in frustration.

I NEVER DID

Object of the game

To speculate on the experiences of other players.

What you need

No special equipment needed.

How to play

This is an excellent game for getting people to reveal their deepest and darkest secrets while under the influence. It is, however, quite difficult to get your head round, so don't wait until people are too under the influence before attempting to explain the rules.

The idea is for players to name something they have never done but which they are pretty sure everybody else in the group has done. The revelation doesn't have to be true, and in fact it probably shouldn't be but, if anyone wants to catch you out, they will have to reveal a truth about themselves. For example, if a player claims "I have never eaten a peanut," he's probably on fairly safe ground since nobody else present will be able to claim the same. But, if he's unlucky and there is somebody present who happens to be chronically allergic to peanuts, that person can speak up and the player who made the claim is out of the game.

Players who can't think of a claim within a pre-decided time span are also eliminated. Claims may also be challenged. For example, the player who claimed that he had never eaten a peanut because of his allergic condition could be challenged on the grounds that he would never have known about his condition unless he had once eaten a peanut. Convincing refutations of challenges should result in a forfeit being required of the challenger.

EVIL TWIN

Object of the game

To act in a way completely contrary to your partner.

What you need

Two hats.

How to play

A very challenging game, but more of a spectator sport than a mucking-in experience. One player is chosen to start and receives both of the hats. Wearing one of them, he or she must place the other one on the head of any other player, who becomes the evil twin.

It is the evil twin's role to do exactly the opposite of the other hat-wearing player. Since it's very difficult to say what the opposite of eating a pretzel is, other guests will frequently be called upon to adjudicate.

WOODLAND ANIMALS

Object of the game

To locate nuts hidden around the house.

What you need

A supply of nuts or sweets.

How to play

This is an extremely silly searching game that challenges players to imitate the noises and mannerisms of wild animals. Before playing you will need to hide twenty or thirty nuts or sweets around the house.

Each player must take on the identity of an animal so, since anyone in their right mind will choose something easy like a dog or a cow, you might want to assign identities by writing them on slips of paper and having players draw them at random. Suitable animals might include a stag, a squirrel, an ape, a snake and an armadillo.

Once every player has been given an animal identity, divide them into equal teams and assign one member of each team as team leader. Give leaders a few minutes to memorize which animals are on their team and to familiarize themselves with the noises they have chosen to make their own.

Players have fifteen or twenty minutes to wander the house, strictly in their animal personas, searching for the hidden nuts. Any player that locates one must draw the attention of his team leader to its location, again while remaining true to the characteristics of their designated animal. Expect hilarious scenes as players imitating dogs yap around the heels of the team leader and those playing snakes attempt to point out hidden nuts using only their tongues.

BOTTLE PASSING

Object of the game

To pass a bottle to team mates using only your knees.

What you need

One empty bottle for each team.

How to play

Yet another variation of a passing-the-object-in-an-awkward-manner style game. In this case, the object to be passed is an empty bottle and the awkward manner is between the knees.

Equal teams should be formed and a bottle given to the first player in each line. With the bottle gripped between their knees, they must attempt to pass it to the next player in line in such a way that they too end up with it held between their knees. Obviously, handling the bottle with any part of the anatomy other than the knees is not allowed. The first team to get the bottle to the end of its team line and back again wins the game.

To enhance the challenge team members could be required to stand several feet apart so that a certain amount of waddling across the floor is needed before the exchange can be effected.

Another option is to use a sealed plastic bottle half-full of water so that the sloshing liquid makes its behaviour less predictable. Bare knees are a definite advantage in this game but, sadly, the short tight skirts that go with them definitely are not.

ACCUMULATION

Object of the game

To remember a sequence of silly actions.

What you need

No special equipment needed.

How to play

Players are ranged in a loose circle, not necessarily standing up, and somebody is chosen to go first. The leader performs a simple action, such as sticking out their tongue, and the next player has to repeat this action and then add another of their own devising. Each player around the circle has to repeat the actions of the players before them, in the correct order, and add a new action of their own.

Failing to perform an action, or getting them in the wrong order, means instant elimination. When a player is eliminated, the next players in line gets to start a new sequence. Suitable actions could include stamping a foot, clapping hands, scratching the head or even poking the previous player in the ribs. Clearly, there is plenty of scope for embarrassing players into dropping out by performing particularly lewd actions.

SLAM

Object of the game

To capture all the cards in the pack.

What you need

A pack of playing cards.

How to play

A fast and frenetic card game not enormously dissimilar to Snap. The key to success here is quick reactions and a willingness to act like an overgrown kid.

Cards are divided equally between all players, or as close to equally as makes no odds, and the first player slaps one down from his pile without looking at it first. Unlike Snap, matching the last card that was laid down isn't the point. Only aces, kings, queens and jacks capture the pile, but it's not quite as simple as that.

If an ace is played every player slams their hand down on top of it. If it's a king, everyone must stand and salute. A queen requires all players to stand up and shout "Good morning madam" and when a jack turns up everybody must leap up and clap their hands above their head. The first player to perform one of these actions at the appropriate time wins all of the cards in the pile. In the case of aces it also tends to earn them severe bruising to the back of the hand. The game ends when one player has won all of the cards.

THIEF

Object of the game

To steal an object from under the nose of a guard.

What you need

An object to be stolen, a chair and a blindfold.

How to play

Discover who among your friends has a sideline as a cat burglar in this stealthy challenge. One player will be required to act as guard for the first round and the game tends to be better if only two or three people play at a time.

Blindfold the player chosen to be the guard, sit him or her on a chair in the centre of the room and place the object to be stolen under the chair. The stealable object could be practically anything from a tin of sardines to a light bulb, as long as it's light enough to be easily lifted and carried away.

The first duo, or trio, of thieves start to creep as stealthily and silently as they can towards the guard. The guard keeps his ears open and, if he hears what he thinks is an approaching thief, he can point in the direction that the sound is coming from and shout "Stop thief!" If the challenge is correct and the guard is pointing directly at a thief, that player is eliminated. After an elimination all other active thieves freeze where they are and the guard keeps his blindfold on while another thief gets ready to begin his run.

Each round of the game ends when either the treasure is success-fully stolen or all thieves are successfully eliminated. Determining what counts as a successful theft is up to you. A good rule is to consider the treasure stolen when somebody manages to carry it a few feet away from the guard, but you could make it harder by requiring that the thief must get back to the edge of the room or easier by counting a finger laid on the treasure as a completed theft. The game ends when everybody has had a go as guard and the winner is the one who has detected the most thieves.

DEAD RATS

Object of the game

To lie very still in the pose of a dead rat.

What you need

No special equipment needed.

How to play

A game that should appeal to pest control operatives and is best played as an ongoing challenge throughout the evening. Inform all guests on arrival that, for the duration of the party, Dead Rats rules apply. This means that, at any point, including during another game, the host can shout "Dead rats!" and all players must immediately drop to the ground and take on the appearance of a deceased rodent with arms and legs stuck up in the air.

The object of the exercise is to lie as still as possible for as long as possible. To reduce the likelihood of half-full wine glasses being tossed across the room as overzealous players hurl themselves to the floor, you should explain that it's the longevity of the pose rather than the speed at which it's achieved that counts. The last player to remain in the dead rat pose wins that round of the game.

Particularly cruel hosts can take advantage of their friends' familiarity with the rules of Dead Rats to play a nasty practical joke at the next party. Simply tell only one or two players that Dead Rats rules apply and then watch with glee as your unfortunate victims throw themselves to the ground the first time you shout the magic words only to discover that everyone else is stood looking down at them with looks of apprehensive bemusement on their faces. It's not nice, but it is extremely funny.

NIGHT IN THE ZOO

Object of the game

To figure out how many animals are present.

What you need

Pen and paper for all guests.

How to play

Before guests arrive, make a list of animals that make a distinctive noise. Suggestions include lion, horse, pig, donkey, sea lion, seagull, cat, mouse, owl, snake, cockerel, bee, frog, goose and dog. Put the name of each animal on a separate slip of paper and jumble them all together in a hat or other receptacle.

Players draw a slip of paper and read it in secret. When all the light go off, each player must wander around making his or her animal noise as loudly as they can. At the same time they should be making a mental note of any other animal noises they can identify.

After a few minutes of this appalling cacophony of howling, growling, croaking and cawing, turn the lights back on and hand each player a sheet of paper and a pen. Players attempt to make a list of all the animals they heard during their "night in the zoo." Check the answers against your initial list and award a prize to the winner.

NOAH'S ARK

Object of the game

To find a mate in the dark.

What you need

Slips of paper and something to put them in.

How to play

In this game, guests get to participate in a re-enactment of scenes of chaos aboard Noah's Ark. Prepare a list of animals with distinctive calls and write them on slips of paper so that there are two slips bearing the name of each animal. Refer to Night in the Zoo for a list of suggestions.

Place the slips of paper into two containers so that each container holds one slip bearing the name of each animal. Have the men draw a slip from one container and the women draw one from the other. Impress on players that the animal they select must remain secret at this stage.

Turn off the lights and let the fun begin. Players with the same animals named on their slips of paper have to locate each other in the dark using only the appropriate animal noise. Once everybody is paired-up, turn on the lights to discover which couples have taken advantage of the situation to cement their partnership further. Buckets of water should be kept to hand.

MUMMIFICATION

Object of the game

To turn your partner into a convincing mummy.

What you need

A roll of toilet paper for each pair.

How to play

An extremely simple game that should appeal to taxidermists and Egyptologists alike. Arrange players into likely pairs and give each couple a toilet roll. Players have three minutes in which to wrap the toilet roll around their partner until they are practically indistinguishable from Egyptian mummies. Traditionally it's the woman who wraps the man, but feel free to throw convention to the wind.

The couple judged to have created the most realistic mummy wins the game. Additional points may be awarded for mummified partners that can perform a classic stiff-legged zombie-like mummy walk with accompanying moans and groans.

RAILWAYS

Object of the game

To roll a ball along two lengths of string.

What you need

Two lengths of string and a ping pong ball for each pair of players.

How to play

Hosts will need to prepare two identical lengths of string (about four feet) for each couple. Players stand face to face, each holding one end of both lengths of string so that the strings are taut between them. Teams need to hold their strings close enough together so that a ping pong ball won't be able to fall through the gap between them.

With ping pong balls in place at one end of each couple's string railway tracks, the game can begin. By raising his or her hands slightly one player in each couple starts the ball rolling along the strings towards their partner. The first couple to get their ball to complete six full lengths of their strings wins the game.

The most critical moment comes when the ball approaches the end of the strings. If it's going too fast it can easily roll over a player's hands and end up on the floor. Balls derailed in this way, or balls that slip between slack or badly spaced strings, must be replaced at the start of that length for another attempt.

DREAMBOATS

Object of the game

To guess which celebrities other players are attracted to.

What you need

A pen and some paper.

How to play

Although only really suitable for a gathering of people who know each other quite well this game could also be used with a group of people who want to get to know each other better. The host takes each guest to one side and asks them to name a celebrity that they wouldn't mind becoming romantically involved with. Armed with a complete list of secret dreamboats the host can start the guessing game.

Start with any player at random. He or she can pick any other player and guess who they think that person would have named as their fantasy love interest. Clearly, this is where knowing the other guests well is a big advantage. If the guess is correct that player drops out and the guesser gets another go. If the guess is incorrect that person gets to make their own suggestion to another player.

It is perfectly legal for players with super-sensitive partners present to name fictional characters, such as Wilma Flintstone or Daphne from Scooby Doo, so be prepared to cast your guessing net widely. The host should keep the original list handy to guard against cheats.

SPINNER

Object of the game

To spin a plate.

What you need

A sturdy plastic plate.

How to play

Seat all players in chairs arranged in a circle and choose one to be the initial plate-spinner. To start the game, the first plate-spinner spins the plate on its edge as rapidly as he can and then calls out the name of another player, preferably one that isn't paying attention. He must now rush to get back to his seat before the plate stops spinning while the player whose name was called must rush to get to the plate.

There are several possible outcomes to this plate-spinning gambit. If the plate-spinner gets back to his seat before the plate stops spinning, and before the player whose name he called can catch it, then that person becomes the new plate-spinner. If the plate stops spinning before he reaches his chair, he remains as plate-spinner. If the called player reaches the plate before it stops spinning but after the plate-spinner has reached his chair, he or she can call on any other player to become the new spinner.

The whole trick to the plate-spinner's job is to ensure that the plate doesn't remain in motion long enough for another player to reach it, but does keep spinning just long enough for him to gain his chair.

VENTRILOQUIST

Object of the game

To speak for your partner.

What you need

No special equipment needed.

How to play

This game can only really be played with a group of established partners or people who know each other extremely well. Form all players, except one, into pairs with the people they know best. The left-over player becomes the game's questioner and should be a person of uncommon wit who can think on their feet.

The questioner's job is to approach a couple and ask one or other of them a question. Here's where the ventriloquism angle come in; the partner of the player that was asked must answer, not the person asked the question.

The questioner's best tactic is to ask a question that he or she knows one partner has the answer to, but to ask it so that the other partner has to reply. Players who answer questions put to them and not their partners get both of them eliminated from the game.

ZOO SNAP

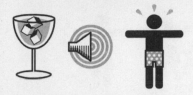

Object of the game

To win all the cards in the pack.

What you need

A pack of playing cards.

How to play

A variation of snap that requires players to make loud and absurd animal noises – clearly a game of considerable sophistication suitable for the classiest of cocktail parties.

Players are given an animal identity, or they can be allowed to choose one of their own as long as everyone chooses a different animal. Any animal can be chosen, as long as it makes a recognizable, and preferably loud, noise. Refer to Night in the Zoo for a list of suitable beasts. Allow players a few minutes to practise their animal noises so that everybody can memorize which player is imitating which animal.

Deal out the cards and play Snap as usual. The difference is this; when a player lays down a card that matches the previous card in the pile, the first person to make that person's animal noise wins the trick. Of course this needn't necessarily be the player who laid the card, anyone can leap in and steal his thunder, as long as they can remember the correct animal noise associated with that player.

SLAVE MARKET

Object of the game

To purchase as many slaves as possible.

What you need

Lots of pennies.

How to play

To get the full flavour of this highly politically incorrect game it should be incorporated into a full-blown Roman banquet theme night, complete with togas, wine fountains and optional orgy. Of course, none of these things are strictly necessary, but it's worth making the effort.

The hardest part of this game is deciding who should act as the slaves and who the slave-buyers. Traditionally the divide is made along male–female lines, with the men and the women taking it in turns to bid for each other, but you can choose any variation on that theme that seems most appropriate.

Line the slaves up on one side of the room, chains optional, while the buyers lounge about on cushions eating grapes off the vine. Buyers should be issued with exactly the same number of pennies each, about twenty or thirty should be sufficient. With the host acting as slave master and auctioneer, the bidding begins with the first slave in the line. The auctioneer should of course talk-up his or her goods to fetch the best price. Buyers continue bidding until they have run out of money, or there are no more slaves left to purchase. The object of the game is to acquire more slaves than any other player.

Theoretically, buyers can do whatever they like with their slaves for the next hour or so but, depending on the moral character of your friends, you might want to have a copy of the International Charter of Human Rights lying around for quick reference.

CHAIN GANG

Object of the game

To form, and dismantle, a chain of paper clips.

What you need

Lots of paper clips.

How to play

A game that involves manipulating fiddly metal objects behind your back, but has nothing to do with bra straps. Still, there's plenty of entertainment to be had that doesn't involve the removal of women's undergarments – or at least that's what numerous women have been heard to claim.

Give each player a paper clip and organize them into two equal teams. Standing shoulder to shoulder with their paper clips held behind their backs, teams are ready to begin the challenge. The first player in each team passes his or her paperclip into the hands of the next player in line who hooks their own clip onto it and passes both to the next player. This continues, all performed behind the backs of the players, until a chain of paper clips reaches the last player in line.

For the return journey along the line of team mates the chain of paper clips is passed in front of the body, but solely by means of elbows. When the starting player receives the chain he puts it behind his back and unhooks one clip before passing it on. When each player in the team can hold up one paper clip, the challenge is over.

THE FLYING GAME

Object of the game

To catch out other players and make them look silly.

What you need

No special equipment, but a zoological encyclopaedia might be useful.

How to play

One person with a nimble mind, or failing that, a pre-prepared list, sits in the centre of a circle formed by other players. To start, he or she announces "My little bird can fly" and then adds another term followed by the word "fly, " such as "Eagles fly!" If the final statement is true, as it is in the case of Eagles, everybody must leap up, flap their arms like mad things and squawk for all they're worth. If the statement isn't true, as in "Lemmings fly!" players should remain seated and silent.

The trick is to try and catch people out with birds such as penguins and kiwis, which cannot fly, and beasts such as squirrels and frogs, some species of which can fly. Anyone who flaps at an animal that can't fly, or fails to flap for one that can, is eliminated. At gatherings of zoologists you might want to play the "My little bird can photosynthesize" variation of the game.

PASS ME A TISSUE

Object of the game

To pass a tissue from straw to straw.

What you need

Tissues and a drinking straw for each player.

How to play

Another cunning variation from the object-passing school of party games. The object to be passed is a tissue and it is transported by the simple expedient of placing it over the end of a drinking draw and sucking in. Passing must be achieved without ripping the team tissue to shreds, a task that requires one player to breathe out just as his team mate breathes in.

Since this passing exercise is quite easy you should require that the tissue be passed up and down the line two or three times before victory can be claimed.

BEAN DIVING

Object of the game

To retrieve a prize from the bottom of a bowl of baked beans.

What you need

A bowl, lots of baked beans and something to clean up with afterwards.

How to play

A variation on bobbing for apples, this game can create one hell of a mess and shouldn't be played by people with an aversion to getting baked beans up their nose.

Simply empty several cans of baked beans into a large bowl and then place a prize, such as a wrapped chocolate or other sweet, at the bottom of the bowl. Players face the task of plunging their faces into the beans in an attempt to retrieve the prize using only their mouths. A less stomach-churning version of the game replaces the bowl of beans with a trough of cornflakes.

TITLE TANGLE

Object of the game

To untangle a film title from unrelated sentences.

What you need

Pens and paper.

How to play

This game requires quite a lot of thought on the part of players, and a pre-prepared list of long film or book titles would also be a good idea.

Each player gets a turn as guesser, so it doesn't really matter who is first to be banished from the room. They may need to be gone for some time, so anyone who needs to make a trip to the smallest room would be a good choice. While the exile is away the other players choose a film or book title, depending on which category you have decided to use, and a sentence is composed for each word of that title. The sentence must contain the relevant word, but in as subtle a way as possible. For example, if the film title chosen was Gone with the Wind, the sentences could look like this:

If she hadn't GONE to Paris, she would never have met him.
WITH a heavy heart, I closed the gate.
Only by unlocking THE chest could I discover what was inside.
Rain driven by a biting WIND made westerly progress difficult.

The key to misleading the guesser is to put in lots of significant-sounding words that actually have nothing to do with the actual title. On first hearing the sentences above, most players will be struggling to think of a film to do with Paris, gates, locked chests or westerly progress. Obviously, some titles are a lot harder to hide than others — Bridge Over the River Kwai for example — so take care in your initial selection.

Allow three or four guesses with diminishing point values so that getting the title right on the first guess earns four point, three points on the second guess, two on the thirds and so on. Allowing guessers to write down the sentences makes the challenge easier. The game can also be played with song or play titles, or with proverbs.

GOOD NEWS, BAD NEWS

Object of the game

To end up with good news rather than bad.

What you need

Two envelopes and two pieces of paper.

How to play

An excellent game that lasts for the duration of the party and should be used to give away the one genuinely valuable or useful prize of the evening. To prepare, write "Good news" on one piece of paper and "Bad news" on the other and seal each one in a separate envelope. The envelopes don't have to be identical, but you must make sure that it's not possible to read what is written on the piece of paper inside, even if held up to a strong light.

Once all guests have arrived, show the envelopes and explain that one of them contains good news, and one bad news. Whoever has the good-news envelope in their possession at the end of the evening wins a prize, but whoever has the bad-news envelope at that point has to perform a horrifyingly embarrassing forfeit. Hand each envelope to a guest at random.

At any point in the evening envelope-holders may attempt to pass their package to any other guest. This can be done openly, or by sneakily slipping it into their pocket. Non-envelope holders are also allowed to beg, borrow or steal envelopes from other players. It's all a question of weighing the risk of forfeit against prize. A few ground rules are probably advisable; putting envelopes in coats or bags left in the hallway should be banned since it doesn't allow the owner a chance to discover that they have been landed with an envelope until it's too late.

TANGLE

Object of the game

To untangle a length of wool in the quickest time.

What you need

A chair for each player and a ball of wool.

How to play

Cut identical lengths of wool for each player – they should be quite long otherwise the challenge is too easy. Take each strand and tangle it around a different chair. The tangle should be as complex as you can make it without involving actual knots.

Each player sits in a different wool-tangled chair and, on the word "Go!" attempts to untangle his strand without getting up. It is vital that at least one buttock remains in contact with the seat of the chair at all times – failure to comply results in disqualification. The first player to completely disentangle the wool from his chair wins the game.

INDOOR FISHING

Object of the game

To hook as many paper-clip fish as possible.

What you need

Paper clips, coat hangers and a large bowl of water.

How to play

Turn the normally relaxed and philosophical art of angling into a wine-fuelled frenzy in the comfort of your own living room. Fill a large bowl with water – a washing-up bowl would be fine but for real class an old aquarium tank is highly desirable. Sprinkle paper clips into the bowl, adding a few extra large ones for that genuine one-that-got-away experience. Serviceable fishing rods can be fashioned by untwisting and straightening out wire coat hangers.

On the command "Fish!" anglers plunge their rods into the waters and attempt to hook as many paper-clip fish as they can in the allotted time (about five minutes should be plenty). If you can be bothered with the preparation involved, multi-coloured plastic coated paper clips can be used, with each colour carrying a different point value.

As has been observed on many occasions, there's a thin line between fishing and standing near a river looking like an idiot. In this case you'll be had pressed to find any kind of line, thin or otherwise.

BOSSES AND SECRETARIES

Object of the game

To take dictation in a noisy room.

What you need

Paper and pens and short newspaper articles.

How to play

Despite its name, this game doesn't involve any after-hours hanky panky or stationery-cupboard trysts. In fact, the secretaries and the bosses need to be kept as far apart as possible.

Form all players into pairs and then let them decide between themselves who gets to be the boss and who the secretary (they can swap for the second round). Bosses stand on one side of the room and secretaries on the other. All bosses are issued with a short piece of text that they will have to try and dictate to their secretaries. Suitable texts might include short newspaper articles, the blurbs on the backs of paperback novels, or letters printed on agony-aunt pages. It is, however, vitally important that all bosses are issued with different texts.

At the command "Dictate!" the line of bosses begin bellowing to their respective secretaries who have the unenviable task of writing down what they think they hear. To add to the fun, have music playing, or even better a talk show on the radio going at full blast. The secretary and boss team with the most accurately dictated text wins the game.

BALLOON TUNNEL

Object of the game

To pass a balloon between your legs while blindfolded.

What you need

Blindfolds for every player and an inflated balloon for each team.

How to play

There is practically no limit to the amount of fun that can be had with blindfolds and inflated balloons, but much of it is far too explicit for these pages so here's a very silly game instead.

Arrange players into the customary two teams and give everyone a blindfold. Team members should line up with their legs akimbo and their heads down. This is probably best done before blindfolds are put in place to minimize unexpected head-buttock collisions. Hand the first player in each line an inflated balloon and blow the whistle.

Quite simply the balloon has to be passed between a player's legs into the hands of the team mate behind. This would probably be fairly simple, if it wasn't for the blindfolds. Lost balloons must be located by players with their blindfolds still firmly in place. The first team to pass their balloon to the last player in line wins the game. This might be a good game to avoid if radishes have been on the menu in the past few hours.

HOT AIR

Object of the game

To prevent a feather from falling onto your body.

What you need

Some feathers.

How to play

Although this game is played from a completely prone position it still requires a great deal of puff if you want to avoid elimination.

To begin, everybody stretches out on their back on the floor. Make everyone shuffle together so they're packed like sardines. Check that no one has fallen asleep and begin the game by tossing two or three feathers into the air above the giggling carpet of bodies.

By puffing with all their might players must attempt to prevent feathers from landing on their bodies. Lifting any part of the body off the floor is illegal, as is shuffling out of the way – although this should be well nigh impossible if players are packed together tightly enough. Any player who ends up as a landing pad for a feather is eliminated. Other players should shuffle together to close any gaps left by eliminations.

DRINKING BIRDS

Object of the game

To drink a bowl of water using a tea spoon.

What you need

A tea spoon and a large bowl for each player.

How to play

This is a straight eating contest, except that competitors race to drink a bowl of water. The catch is that the bowl must remain on the table while water is transported to the mouth by means of a teaspoon. The first player to scoop every last drop of liquid from his or her bowl wins the game, and the right to be first in the queue for the bathroom.

This is an excellent game to get people sobered up if wine is getting a bit too much. Alternatively, you could use wine instead of water for exactly the opposite effect.

TELL THE TRUTH

Object of the game

To tell the truth.

What you need

No special equipment.

How to play

If George Washington really did never tell a lie he must have been an extremely annoying and unpleasant guest at parties, as this game will soon reveal.

The premise is very simple; players must undertake to speak only the truth in answer to any question put to them. Even ignorance is not an excused, when asked the question "Do you think Harold is having an affair with Margery?" you cannot simply claim that you don't know, you have to give your honest opinion.

Since this can be such a harrowing challenge it's often a good idea to follow it with a round of Don't Tell the Truth, in which players are sworn to answer each and every question put to them with a bare-face lie. This can actually be a lot harder than it sounds. In either version of the game, players successfully challenged on their truths or lies should be required to perform a forfeit.

ACCUSATIONS

Object of the game

To guess the identity of your accuser.

What you need

A chair, a pen and some paper.

How to play

If you have ever wanted to accuse your friends of outrageous and immoral acts but were too afraid of libel actions or flying fists to go through with it, this game offers the opportunity to impugn with anonymity.

Each guest takes it in turn to be cast into the outer darkness of the hallway while the host goes around the other players and collects scandalous accusations about the exile. The accusations can be as real or imagined as people care to make them. Once a full charge sheet has been written up, the accused is called in and required to sit in a chair surrounded by the other players. If you can arrange it, a Gestapo-style interrogation lamp adds a nice touch.

The host now acts as chief prosecutor and puts each of the accusations to the chair-bound prisoner in turn. Judging purely by the nature of the charges, he or she must guess who made which accusation. The player who manages to identify the majority of his or her accusers wins the game and an early parole.

JEKYLL AND HYDE

Object of the game

To pander to the best, and worst, aspects of your character.

What you need

No special equipment needed, but professional counselling might be needed later.

How to play

Another wickedly simple role-playing game that can have some very surprising results. An excellent inhibition loosener, but hosts should be warned that, with a few glasses of wine inside them, players have been known to go a bit far.

Divide guests into a Devil team and an Angel team. It's the job of the Devils to be as mean, spiteful, villainous and mischievous as they can while the Angels attempt to remain paragons of piety and understanding in the face of their endless hard-heartedness.

Encourage Devils to be as wicked as they want, but point out that this is just a game and doesn't come with any kind of immunity from prosecution. After half an hour of torture, the Angels get their revenge as the teams switch personas.

WISH LIST

Object of the game

To identify people by their aspirations.

What you need

Slips of paper and pens.

How to play

Each player is equipped with a slip of paper and a pen and required to write answers to the following two questions: "What would you most like to do?" and "What would you most like to do at this moment?" Guests should be encouraged to be as honest as possible and it should be pointed out that players who write "Go home" in response to the second question will be required to do just that.

After everyone has had a few minutes to come up with answers, all slips are folded, collected and redistributed to random participants. Each player must, in turn, read out the answer to the first question and, where possible, carry out the act described in answer to the second. Once all wishes have been vicariously fulfilled, there is a round of guessing to try and match answers to players.

PLOTTERS

Object of the game

To induce paranoia and fear in guests.

What you need

A darkened room.

How to play

A chilling exercise in story telling, this game has been known to make people seriously consider moving to another country and getting a new set of friends.

Make the room as dark as possible before playing to ensure maximum spookiness. Each player takes it in turn to describe, in chilling detail, how they would commit the perfect murder with somebody present in the role of victim. Encourage players to use their knowledge of the personal habits of their intended victim and make sure they cover such details as method, hoped for suffering and means of disposing of the corpse.

MINUTE MARCH

Object of the game

To pace yourself so that you walk across the room in exactly one minute.

What you need

A stop watch or clock with a second hand.

How to play

A very simple but strangely compelling game that tests players' sense of timing. All players start on one side of the room with their heels against the skirting. At the word "Go!" they attempt to walk, or more likely shuffle, across the room in exactly one minute. Obviously, the host must have his or her eye on a watch but all other clocks, watches, sundials or egg timers present must be confiscated or covered.

After exactly a minute the host announces a halt and the player who is closest to his or her destination wins the game. Players who arrive at the far side of the room before the minute is up are disqualified, even if they're just a few seconds early.

SDRAWKCAB

Object of the game

To recite the alphabet backwards.

What you need

No special equipment needed.

How to play

Another game with simple rules but a high level of difficulty. Everybody stands in a circle and attempts to recite the alphabet backwards, taking turns, with the first player starting at "Z." Hesitating or giving the wrong letter results in that player being eliminated from the circle.

After a while, if nobody is making any mistakes, continue around the circle but omit vowels. To add another level of difficulty, omit all letters that have only vertical and horizontal straight lines in their printed form (e.g. L, T, I, L, H, F).

HUMAN KNOT

Object of the game

To untangle a pile of writhing party guests.

What you need

Broad-minded friends.

How to play

People with inhibitions about invasion of their personal space should definitely steer clear of this game. This takes the legendary party favourite Twister to new and shocking heights.

One player is chosen to be the outcast and is required to leave the room. Anyone with a tricky back or a fresh plaster cast would be a good choice. Everyone else forms a circle and joins hands. Without releasing hold of each other, the circled players form themselves into a twisted, heaving tangle of bodies by ducking under arms, crawling through legs and generally getting up close and personal.

Once the tangle has settled down into a stable form, the exiled player is brought back into the room. After he finishes laughing, it becomes his job to try and untangle the mess and return the ring to its original form. Once again, players in the morass are not allowed to release their grip on their neighbours' hands during the unscrambling process.

NOT IN FRONT OF THE CHILDREN

Let's face it, most people go to parties not for the stimulating conversation of intelligent acquaintances but for the opportunity to make friends with members of the opposite sex. Parties are ideal occasions to step out of the boring hush puppies of everyday social conventions and into the glittering heels of delicious wickedness. If you want a swinging party but aren't prepared to go so far as to have a swingers' party, try some of these impish challenges.

MORPH

Object of the game

To get into your partner's trousers.

What you need

Fully-clothed guests.

How to play

Although a physical game, this is a challenge that requires a fair amount of lateral thinking, and the ability to balance on one leg for at least part of the time, so any attempt to play after guests have polished of a half-dozen bottles of Chardonnay is likely to result in sheer chaos rather than actual competition.

Pair players off in such a way that the resulting couples are on fairly intimate terms, or at least don't openly despise one another – this is a cooperative game after all. Standing around the room with plenty of space between them, paired players are faced with the seemingly simple task of swapping clothes with their partners. The confounding factor, however, is that they must remain in some form of physical contact with that partner at all times. This can be anything from a multi-limbed embrace to coy hand-holding or Inuit-style nose rubbing.

Clearly, there is scope here for things to get very naughty indeed, not to say unhygienic, so you should probably draw a line at underwear swapping. The first couple to successfully swap clothes without losing physical contact wins the game. Pairs that end up hopelessly entangled in each other's rigging may have to be cut free at this point, unless they are enjoying the experience.

Although this sounds like a fairly frenetic game, in practice the only hope for success is to take things slowly and to think several steps ahead before acting. This makes it an ideal chill-out interlude before proceeding with more hectic activities. Of course, there is always the danger that several couples will suddenly remember that they "left the gas on" and rush off home after a round of such embarrassment.

BOTTOMS UP

Object of the game

To identify players by their spanking technique.

What you need

A blindfold and a chair.

How to play

You may not think of yourself as an S & M type, but this game is guaranteed to raise a glassy-eyed smile from all but the terminally repressed. It really is quite naughty, so take care to suggest it only in company that is sure to be appreciative.

Essentially, this is a risqué version of Blind Man's Buff – a game notorious for the ease with which it can be subverted by partygoers with one-track minds. In this variation, players attempt to identify each other not from disguised voices or chaste fingertip feeling but by vigorous spanking.

Choose one player to be blindfolded and have them bend over the chair in a comfortable position. Other players take it in turns to deliver open-handed blows onto the rump of the beleaguered guest. Slaps can vary in severity from full-blooded wallops, to appreciative taps, to barely concealed caresses. While enduring this sequence of strikes all the blindfolded player has to do is identify the people who are delivering them. A correct guess results in the spanker becoming the spanked for the next round.

UNDERCOVER

Object of the game

To horribly embarrass a guest.

What you need

A large blanket.

How to play

This is really a practical joke rather than a game and, as such, can only be performed on a victim once. Make sure you choose someone who will see the funny side, eventually at least. It also requires most, if not all, of the rest of those present to be in on the joke.

Seat your dupe on the floor and cover him or her with a large blanket. The blanket must be large enough to allow the person underneath to move around without revealing themselves prematurely. At this point the victim is informed that the other players have in mind something that he has "On his person," and that he must pass articles out from under the blanket until he gets to the right one.

Most victims, unless they are unashamed naturalists, will begin tentatively by removing a shoe or a watch or an earring until forced to move on to move vital elements of clothing such as trousers or skirts by the failure of these to meet with the group's approval. Continue refusing to accept the offered articles of clothing until your reluctant striptease artist has no choice but to remove items that seriously compromise standards of public decency.

It's entirely up to you how far you allow the torture to continue. There is no reason why the game can't continue until the victim is in such a state of undress that they have to start considering removing clumps of hair. Of course the victim will come to suspect fairly early on that the group has no particular item in mind, but you can truthfully assure them that this is not the case — the item you have in mind is the blanket itself.

PERFECT TEN

Object of the game

To act as passionately as a playing card dictates.

What you need

A pack of playing cards.

How to play

A game based on the kind of quizzes found in women's and men's magazines that ask searching questions such as "How satisfied are you with your lover's body?" and require answers in the form of a rating from one to ten. Before play can begin you will need to remove all the picture cards from the pack of playing cards so you are left with only those cards marked one to ten.

Divide all players into couples using one of the couple-forming games in the icebreakers section of this book or, alternatively, allow them to pair-off according to preference. Go from pair to pair with the denuded pack of cards and allow each player to choose one card. Cards should be kept secret even from partners.

Once everybody has a card, the fun can begin. Each couple in turn has to act out their passion for each other based on the numerical value on their cards. So, an ace would translate as barely concealed contempt while a ten would indicate an overwhelming desire to be alone with their partner. If you are lucky enough to get a pairing that holds a one and a ten the results can be highly amusing. Beware of couples with two tens, they tend to suddenly decide they have to leave in a hurry or not want to play the game any more.

If sheer entertainment value isn't enough, the game can be made competitive by having players attempt to guess the cards held by each couple.

BLIND MAN'S KISS

Object of the game

To identify players by their kissing style.

What you need

A blindfold and a handy supply of breath mints.

How to play

It's difficult to imagine a less subtle variation of Blind Man's Buff than this so it's probably best left until a stage of the evening when subtlety has followed inhibition straight out of the window.

Arrange players into the familiar circle and place a blindfolded volunteer in the centre. While the player in the middle twists and spins in any manner he or she desires, the circle of other guests orbits around in a suitably giggly and prancing manner. At any moment the blind man can stop the merry dance by standing still, or as still as they are able, and pointing directly outwards.

The pointed-at player tip-toes up to the blind man and delivers a full kiss on the lips, attempting to disguise their identity as well as they are able by stooping, stomping, simpering, guffawing or otherwise acting in an uncharacteristic manner. If the kissed blind man correctly guesses the identity of the kisser, that player takes a turn in the centre of the circle.

Some players have been known to exhibit an extreme reluctance to give up the role of blind man, especially when the male–female mix of other guests is stacked in their favour, so you might want to set a four- or five-kiss limit to ensure everyone gets a go. It's also a good idea to ban any form of bodily contact other than lip-to-lip to avoid overly familiar couples bringing the proceedings to a halt while they relive more private occasions involving blindfolds.

CROSS-DRESS DASH

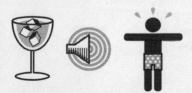

Object of the game

To dress as quickly as possible.

What you need

An assortment of men's and women's clothing.

How to play

This game takes advantage of the perennially hilarious concept of men wearing women's clothing. Male players should take care over the degree of enthusiasm or skill they exhibit during this challenge unless they are already acknowledged cross-dressers.

You will need to provide one full outfit of female clothing for each male player, and one full outfit of male clothing for each female player. Pile the clothes in two gender-specific heaps and line up players in same-sex groups on the other side of the room. At the starting pistol the men make a dash for the women's clothing while the women streak towards the men's. The word "streak" here could of course be taken literally since, in its purest and sauciest form, this game should begin with players wearing as little as possible.

However far you decide to go in setting a dress code for starting conditions, the end result is the same. Players must attempt to put on one full costume of clothes before racing back to the start position. Exactly what comprises an outfit will depend on how many clothes you are able to assemble for the game, but it should include at least five or six items. The first player from each group that makes it back wearing all the correct clothes on roughly the right parts of the body wins the game.

If you're feeling sneaky, make sure there aren't quite enough clothes to go round. That way you get to watch full-grown men grappling with each other for possession of the last pair of frilly knickers or demure girlfriends liberating size twelve brogues with extreme prejudice.

NECKING GAME

Object of the game

To pass on a piece of fruit.

What you need

An orange for each team.

How to play

A classic party game that owes its reputation for sauciness purely to the way in which it brings players into kissing distance.

Divide players into two equal teams and arrange them in boy-girl-boy-girl rows (or whatever takes your fancy). The first player in each row begins by placing an orange so that it is held between chin and upper chest. Without using any other part of the body, specifically the hands, he or she must then attempt to pass it to the next player in line so that they too end up holding the orange in the same manner.

Players continue passing the fruit in this fashion until it gets to the last player in their team line, who must hold it for five seconds. Since it's practically impossible to retrieve a dropped orange using your chin, teams guilty of losing their fruit should be required to start again from the beginning.

Super-saucy hosts may be interested in replacing the orange with ticklish items to add a new element to the game.

TABLOIDS

Object of the game

To compose a saucy tabloid headline.

What you need

No special equipment needed but pen and paper might come in handy.

How to play

One player starts the proceedings by shouting out one word that could conceivable be found in a tabloid headline – something like "KNICKERS" or "ROMP" or "NOOKIE" should fit the bill nicely. The next player adds a word before or after that supplied by his journalistic colleague to form something like "KNICKERS LOST" or "SECRET ROMP" or "NOOKIE SHOP." Hosts might want to note down these words as they are provided.

Players continue adding words until things reach a natural conclusion with fully-rounded gems of tabloid journalese such as "ASTRONAUTS KNICKERS LOST IN SPACE" or "MY SECRET ROMP WITH SEX-STARVED NETBALL TEAM" or "NOOKIE SHOP DISCOVERED OVER VICAR'S DROP-IN CENTRE."

TABLOID CONSEQUENCES

Object of the game

To create a random tabloid headline.

What you need

Pen and paper.

How to play

Tabloid journalists are notorious for their lack of regard for the consequences of their actions, a fact that this game cheerfully acknowledges and turns into a form of entertainment – this can be seen as a chilling indictment of modern standards of morality, or as a lucky coincidence, depending on your degree of cynicism.

As with a regular game of Consequences, the end result is achieved by having players contribute one word or term without knowing what the previous word or term happened to be. Player one begins by writing on the top of a sheet of paper and then passing it on to the next player. Player two adds his or her entry and then folds the paper over so that the first entry cannot be seen before passing the paper on. Each player should fold so that only their entry is visible to the next contributor.

For the end result to make any kind of sense the following rules should be followed:

First entry: An adjective.
Second entry: A noun.
Third entry: A verb.
Fourth entry: The object of the verb.
Fifth entry: A location or another verb.

With any luck you should end up with results along the lines of "RABID NUDISTS ACCUSE PERVERT OF FENCE BREACH" to which the time-honoured by-line "Police looking into it" can be attached.

Players should of course be aware that they are aiming for a tabloid-type headline and be encouraged to use suitable phrases. Classic examples of journalese that you might want to quote to get players in the mood include "KISS-AND-TELL," "ROMP," "TRACK RECORD," "RED-FACED," "BRONZED" and "LOVE-RAT."

SCRUM

Object of the game

For teams to force their way across a line.

What you need

Lots of space and a length of string or rope.

How to play

If you've ever fancied staging a riot but can't be bothered with washing tear gas out of your clothes, this is the next best thing. Probably the most physical and potentially injurious game in this collection, it should only be attempted in a room completely cleared of obstructions or, better still, outside on nice springy grass. Its presence in this section of the book is justified only by the ample opportunity it affords for seemingly innocent groping of and grappling with members of the opposite sex.

The game itself is a kind of reversed tug-of-war in that teams attempt to push rather than pull each other out of the way. Set up a dividing line by securing a length of rope or string to the floor and divide players into two teams of roughly equal shunting power rather than number. The teams face each other across the string arranged in ranks of three or four players. The front rank of each team places their hands on the shoulders of the front rank of the opposing team and, when the whistle blows, everybody begins heaving forward with all their might. The first team to get all its members across the line wins the game.

It should be emphasized that the front ranks aren't allowed to grapple with each other in any way other than by pushing continually at the opposition's chests or shoulders. It should also be emphasized that for maximum enjoyment a strict undress code should apply.

KISSING TRAIN

Object of the game

To kiss as many people as possible.

What you need

A blindfold.

How to play

The joy of this game is that it confounds pleasant expectations only to fulfil them many times over at a later stage. It's a kind of trick, so it can only be played with the same group of people once.

One player, who knows how the game works but has been sworn to secrecy, begins a conga-like line by selecting any other player that he or she likes the look of. The selected player is swiftly blindfolded and the pair proceed around the room – follower with hands around the waist of leader – to suitably inane music until the principal leads his or her victim out of the room.

Once out of sight, the leader delivers a sharp slap to the rump of his or her surprised follower who, given the name of the game, is expecting an entirely different form of physical contact. At this point the blindfold is removed, or possibly is torn off in outrage, and the leader explains the joke, which is this: when players first join the line they receive a slap, but on every subsequent occasion that the line leaves the room they receive a kiss. Self-esteem restored, the victim is led back into the room grinning like an idiot and gets to select the next passenger for the train. He or she of course receives a slap from the original follower who gets the long-awaited kiss from the leader.

As the line gets longer the comedic effect increases as blindfolded players are able to hear the kisses proceeding down the line before themselves receiving a totally unexpected bottom bashing.

RUMOUR MILL

Object of the game

To identify the rumour mongers.

What you need

Pen and paper.

How to play

A spicy version of the game called Accusations in which players
accuse each other of heinous crimes. In this variation juicy titbits of
gossip, true or otherwise, are levelled against each player in turn.

One player is selected to be ostracized and is sent into the outer
darkness of the hallway while the others gather around and share
their tales of imagined skeletons in the cupboard or flagrant
infidelities about him or her. The rumours can be as genuine
or as fanciful as players wish to make them, but they should all be
carefully noted down.

After enduring five minutes of sheer terror as he or she listens to
the gales of laughter coming from the other side of the door, the
outcast is let back into the fold. Once they are seated uncomfortably in the centre of the room, the list of rumours is read out one
face-reddening item at a time. Between taking deep gulps and
fighting back the urge to scream defensive refutations, the accused
attempts to guess which one of his or her former friends voiced
which rumour. One point is scored for every correct guess.

The most easily guessed rumour mongers are the ones who reveal
genuine information, information that only they would know.
Consequently, any player who is able to identify all of his or her
detractors may win the game easily but will never be able to show
their face in public again.

SAUCY WORD-CHAINS

Object of the game

To construct a list of saucy words.

What you need

No special equipment needed.

How to play

A game that panders to people's need to blurt out rude words when under the influence of alcohol. Like other word-chain games, the idea is for each player to come up with a word that begins with the last letter of the previous player's word. Unlike other word-chain games the more off-colour the words are the better.

Player one begins the proceeding by casually casting, for example, "Pants" into the fray – the word that is, not an actual article of clothing. Since "Pants" incontrovertibly ends with the letter "S," the next player could legally counter with "Striptease," to which the next in line would feel obliged to answer with "Erogenous." These are of course fairly tame examples, but in the privacy of your own home you can be as foul-mouthed as you like.

Challenges may be issued at any point if someone feels that a word is not suitably erotic. For example, the word-chain "Lust, Twins, Stroking, Gordon" could be brought to a screeching halt on the grounds that "Gordon" isn't a remotely sensual name. Only by admitting that he or she finds TV wine connoisseur Jilly Gordon immensely attractive could a player so challenged escape elimination from the game.

The game continues until only one player is left to claim victory or until the entire affair degenerates into a pants-bottoms-knickers charade – unless you like that kind of thing.

IN THE END

Object of the game

To create a tale with a saucy ending.

What you need

Pens and paper all round.

How to play

A game that relies on mental titillation rather than the chance to glimpse or fondle other players' underwear may seem less appealing at first but can safely be guaranteed to get pulses racing and giggles flowing just as effectively as its more down-to-earth counterparts.

Before the party you will need to prepare a suitably risqué story ending for each player. The emphasis should be on climaxes featuring embarrassingly ludicrous predicaments rather than out and out pornography. Here are a few examples to set you on the right road:

"Just then, the string broke and I was left with my trousers around my ankles standing in front of the Chief Constable."

"And that's how I came to be found in the under stairs cupboard wearing nothing but a codpiece and a feather boa."

"The next thing I knew the maid was on her knees and all thoughts of an expedition to the Post Office had gone out of the window."

Pass an ending to each player, equip them with pen and paper, and give them five minutes to come up with a plausible tale that could precede these shock endings. Stories can be straightforwardly rude or the suggestive ending can be explained away as the result of an unlikely but perfectly innocent chain of events in the best traditions of bedroom farce. Award laurels to the player who pens the most inventive narrative.

LICK ALONG THE LINE

Object of the game

To smear your team mates with food and then lick it off.

What you need

Whipped cream, chairs and a spoon for each team.

How to play

This game takes the erotically charged concept of spreading whipped cream onto skin and then licking it off but accelerates the process to such an extent that it becomes more Keystone Cops than Nine-and-Half Weeks. This one can definitely get messy so don't play it on expensive carpets or with guests attired in their dry-clean-only best.

Divide players into teams of about five or six. As will become clear, the larger the teams the more challenging and potentially saucy the game begins. Seat team members on rows of chairs and give the first player in each team a bowl of whipped cream and a spoon. At the starting gun, this player leaps from his or her chair and deposits a dollop of cream somewhere on the exposed skin of the next player in line. Team leaders continue down their team lines scooping cream onto their team mates. Each dollop of cream must be placed on bare skin and each must be placed in a different position on the body.

On reaching the end of the line, the first player retraces his or her steps but this time licking the cream off team mates. When this potentially pleasant task has been completed the cream is passed to the next in line for a repeat performance. Continue until all players have smeared and licked each other.

JUNGLE DRUMS

Object of the game

To guide others players into performing risqué tasks.

What you need

Drums, saucepans, buckets or any other objects that can be beaten to make a noise, and a blindfold.

How to play

A variation on the children's game in which players shout "Getting warmer!" or "Getting colder!" to help guide someone to a hidden object. In this version players beat drums, saucepans or other noise-making objects with increasing or decreasing intensity depending on how close or far from the desired objective the blindfolded victim is.

The term "victim" is applicable here because the objective towards which he or she is being urged is likely to result in no small personal embarrassment. Obviously the player to be blindfolded should be out of the room when his or her task is decided on. Suitable assignments are best restricted to pre-arranged categories known to all players such as kissing, pinching, slapping, hugging or patting.

For example, it could be decided that the first player should be directed to slap a girl that everyone knows he has been pursuing unsuccessfully for months. When the victim enters the room he is informed that he is on a slapping mission, but the intended target isn't mentioned. As he lurches around the room, slapping hand at the ready, everyone beats frantically on their makeshift drums as he gets close to his target, finally creating a plaster-loosening barrage of sound as the slap itself becomes imminent.

It should be fairly obvious by this stage that playing this game is nowhere near as fun as watching it, but everyone should be required to take a turn with the blindfold as payment for all the free entertainment.

KISSING LOTTERY

Object of the game

To pick numbers that will result in pleasurable kisses.

What you need

No special equipment required.

How to play

This game is little more than an excuse for guests to kiss each other under the flimsiest of pretexts and is therefore ideal for parties packed with single guests who like nothing better than acting under flimsy pretexts.

Assign a secret number to each player, odd numbers to the men and even numbers to the women. Numbers should be consecutive in the sense that, if there are fourteen women present and eleven men, no woman should have a number higher than twenty-eight and no man should have a number higher than twenty-one. Make sure everyone knows what the maximum numbers are and that women's numbers are even and men's are odd.

Choose one player to start and arrange everyone else in a circle around the brave volunteer. The player in the middle calls out two numbers and the players who have been assigned those numbers rush to kiss him or her – it's entirely up to preference whether people choose to call out numbers for their own or for the opposite sex. Either way, the first player to plant their lips takes over the coveted position in the centre of the circle.

In the early stages of the game, when nobody knows anybody else's number, the player in the centre relies entirely on luck to achieve a longed-for result. Men who happen to call out the number of an ex-girlfriend and a present partner at the same time might be well advised to keep their hands strategically positioned to block any incoming knees. Later on of course, players will start to remember each other's numbers and the resulting calls, as well as the speed or reluctance with which they are responded to, can be immensely revealing.

ANONYMOUS FEET

Object of the game

To identify people by their feet.

What you need

A large sheet rigged to act like a screen and a pen and some paper.

How to play

This is a toned-down version of an extremely naughty game in which players attempt to identify each other from certain distinctive parts of their anatomy, the specifics of which can be left entirely to the imagination of readers.

Divide guests into two roughly equal teams and send one team out of the room while members of the other remove shoes, socks, stockings and any other form of footwear that they may have on. These players then position themselves behind a screen so that only their naked feet are visible.

On re-entering the room the opposing team has a maximum of five minutes in which to correctly identify the owners of the protruding feet. Actually touching feet is prohibited on the grounds that it tends to produce shrieks of ticklish laughter, which can give the game away. Guesses should be meticulously noted down by an independent party, then the screen can be lifted to reveal all. At this point teams change places and the grisly parade of corns, verrucas and untrimmed toenails begins again.

FANTASY ISLAND

Object of the game

To reveal your secret fantasies in public.

What you need

Pens and paper all round.

How to play

This is one of those games that seems like a good idea at the time but can cause toe-curling embarrassment when you wake up the following morning. Install a few secret cameras and microphones in your home before playing and you'll have your friends by the short and curlies for the rest of their lives.

Hand out pens and paper to all players and ask them to write down their secret fantasies while assuring them, almost truthfully, that their identities will remain secret. Fantasies should be restricted to the immediate surroundings and the present company and must involve the player as an active participant – you're not allowed to write something like "My fantasy is to see the host performing a striptease to the soundtrack of The Wizard of Oz."

Collect the sheets of paper, shuffle them thoroughly and redistribute them randomly amongst the players. Players are required to act out as much of the secret fantasy they have been handed as they dare, as long as it doesn't contravene certain sections of the criminal code or the laws of physics. Of course it's possible that a player will receive his or her own fantasy, in which case they have an ideal opportunity to act it out while at the same time appearing shocked and horrified that anyone could have thought of such an unthinkable thing.

Once all the fantasies have been performed, or as many of them as anybody will dare to take on, players attempt to guess who was the author of which fantasy. Guests are under no obligation to own up to their fantasies but, hopefully, the inhibition loosening qualities of the acting-out round will allow the revelations to flow freely.

MODEL OBSERVATION

Object of the game

To pay close attention to the catwalk.

What you need

Two volunteer models, lots of clothes and accessories and pens and paper all round.

How to play

A fairly straightforward observation game for people who like to dress up and know their holdalls from their handbags. Its inclusion in this section is due entirely to the fact that it involves a semi-clad model, a feature that may perk up players' interest no end. You will need two volunteer models; a woman who knows how to wear clothes, and a man who isn't embarrassed to parade around in his underwear. These roles can of course be reversed depending on personal preference.

Players are seated around a makeshift catwalk, or at least a vacuumed strip of carpet, and are told to observe the first model as closely as possible. On cue, the fully clothed model strolls out and struts his or her stuff. This model should be wearing as much as possible and be kitted out with as many accessories as you can muster. After no more than a minute the putative Naomi Campbell retreats and players are handed pen and paper on which to note down as many items of apparel they can remember.

The second model makes his or her entrance after a similar build-up but is of course wearing no more than a t-shirt and shorts. This time the challenge is to guess what the model will be wearing when he or she has actually managed to get dressed. After two minutes, or however long it takes for the model to get into their clobber, there is a repeat performance, but this time fully clothed. The selected outfit can be unusual or simply elegant depending on how much of a show-off you are. Once the show is over, lists are compared and a winner determined.

BUTTOCKS

Object of the game

To transport coins using buttocks only.

What you need

Lots of coins and a couple of dishes.

How to play

Reputed to be a favourite of the crowned heads of Europe for time immemorial, this game derives much of its comedic value from imagining the residents of Balmoral engaging in a session of it after Christmas luncheon.

The idea, such as it is, is for players to transport coins from one end of the room to the other by clenching them between their buttocks. At the start position coins may be positioned using hands but, from that point onwards, only buttocks may be used to hold them in place. At the other end of the room is a dish into which the coins should be deposited. The player who manages to transport the most coins and drop them into a dish within the five-minute time limit wins the game.

For maximum buttock-gripping strength players' posteriors would really have to be bare, but it's unlikely that you will be able to persuade guests to go that far. Trousers and skirts of thick material significantly impeded natural buttock-gripping potential, however, so underpants would be a good practical compromise. Large coins, such as fifty and two pence pieces are easier to handle than small fiddly ones.

TONGUES WILL WAG

Object of the game

To pass a peanut from tongue to tongue.

What you need

Peanuts or small sweets that don't melt in the mouth.

How to play

A game likely to produce shrieks of horror in some quarters and coos of delight in others. Unless guests are particularly inebriated, this can only really be played by people who are already on fairly intimate terms.

Divide players into teams of four or five and have them stand in rows. The first player in each team is given a peanut or a small boiled sweet, which he or she places on the tip of the tongue. From this point onwards the peanut cannot be touched by human hands and must make its journey from one end of the line to the other from tongue to tongue.

Peanuts that are put beyond use by being swallowed or dropped and ground into the carpet should be replaced, but the guilty team will have to start again from the beginning. Team mates who seem to have become distracted from the task in hand and who are performing altogether more intimate tongue manipulations may have to be separated by force. The first team to convey the peanut successfully to the end of their line wins the game and a slightly soggy peanut.

BANANA SPLIT

Object of the game

To guide a banana through a pair of trousers.

What you need

Bananas and guests wearing trousers.

How to play

This game provides one of life's rare opportunities to legitimately use the phrase "Is that a banana in your pocket, or are you just pleased to see me?" There can be few more compelling reasons than that to give something a go but, for male guests, this is anyway probably the most fun that can be had in a public setting without infringing local bylaws.

Divide players into male–female pairs and provide each one with a banana. For reasons that will become obvious, it's not a good idea to use overripe fruits for this game. At the command "Go!" the men stand with their legs apart in a macho stance while their female partners attempt to propel the banana up the inside of one trouser leg and down the other.

It becomes clear at this point why mushy brown bananas are not a good idea. The descent down the second trouser leg is usually the easiest part of the journey while the short but tricky stretch across the top is undoubtedly the most enjoyable, for the man at least. Men may not aid the progress of the banana in any way and flies must remain firmly fastened. As an added challenge, men could be required to keep their hands on their heads at all times – not as easy as it sounds when someone is manipulating your crutch.

The first team to complete this traumatic experience wins the game and a slightly worse for wear banana. Choosing a smaller object to manipulate will increase the difficulty level – if you really want your guests to suffer the embarrassment.

THE DATING GAME

Object of the game
To identify your dream date.

What you need

Pens and paper all round.

How to play

A game not a million miles distant from a certain long-running television programme that also has the word "Date" in the title. The terrifying difference here is that the dream date partner eventually selected will probably be someone you've known and despised for years rather than a handsome stranger.

Select two volunteers, a man and a woman, to be the initial contestants and have them write three pertinent questions that they would put to a prospective dream-date candidate. These should be something along the lines of "Where would you take me for the perfect first date?" or "What do you do to amuse yourself when there's nobody else around?" or "Do you believe in sex before the lights are switched off?"

Have all the men write witty answers to the women's questions and all the women write cheeky answers to the men's questions, or whatever variation suits the circumstances. When this is done, read out the answers to one set of questions or the other, without revealing their authors, and have that candidate select the ones he or she finds most enticing. Only at this point should the identity of the answer writer be revealed to the horror and consternation, or pleasure and delight, of the contestant. Repeat the process for the other contestant.

At this point the event can be rounded of by having the newly-formed couple select one of three envelopes, two of which should contain embarrassing forfeits while the other contains a genuine prize such as "A free trip for two to the local shops to buy more wine." The game can of course be repeated as many times as you wish with new contestants for each round.

STRIP SWAP

Object of the game

To change clothes with your partner.

What you need

Fully-clothed guests and a room that can be completely darkened.

How to play

A very simple game that trades on the erotic frisson of being discovered half-undressed when the lights go on. Needless to say, this is an activity that will require guests to be extensively "loosened up" before it seems like a good idea.

Form players into male–female pairs bearing in mind that they will eventually end up wearing each others clothes – it might be a tad unfair for example to team a diminutive lass with a hulking seven-foot brute with a beer belly, even if they are the best of friends. After the necessary horse-trading, scatter couples so that they have their own space in the room and switch off the lights.

Couples have exactly two minutes to swap as many clothes as they can before the lights are switched back on. It's entirely up to individual tastes and competitive spirits how far players can go in this process. Points are awarded for every item of clothing swapped so that extra two points for exchanged underwear could make the crucial difference between winning and losing.

To save at least a modicum of decency it's probably a good idea to have a ten-second count down before the lights go on again. Of course, flicking the light switch on and off at random intervals would be an inexcusable betrayal of trust on the part of a host — wouldn't it?

POSTMAN'S KNOCK

Object of the game

To be kissed.

What you need

A room with a door.

How to play

An adult party classic, this game has gained its status as a perennial favourite because it's simple, cheap and delivers the desired results — odd that such characteristics should be associated with the postal service.

Choose a volunteer from amongst the many clamouring to go first and bestow on them the honorary title of postman, postmistress or postperson depending on prevailing levels of political correctness in your immediate area. Escort the postman outside while the other players choose numbers.

The numbering process can be as simple as lining everyone up and assigning numbers sequentially regardless of sex, or as complicated as assigning odd numbers to one sex and even numbers to the other. In the first case, the postman will have no idea whether he is calling on a man or a woman, which can be disappointing, whereas in the second case the postman will be able to follow his natural preference, which is more fulfilling but also time consuming.

Either way, the postman's job is to knock loudly on the door and announce "I have a special delivery for number fourteen," or whatever number springs to mind. The player whose number corresponds to that called out by the postman trips merrily to the door, opens it and receives a kiss from the horrified or delighted postal worker on the other side. The kissed player becomes the next postal operative.

Ideally, players should change numbers for every new postman, which is why the straightforward consecutive numbering system is easiest. As a rule, it's better to have the postman come into the room rather than to have the called player go out. That way other players can check that undesirable kisses have been properly delivered and that desirable ones don't go on so long that everyone else gets bored.

THREADS

Object of the game

To thread team members together.

What you need

One large key and a long length of string for each team.

How to play

The apparatus for this game is important, so you should spend some time getting it right. The string needs to be strong and the key must be tied securely to one end. A large Chubb lock type key is best or, alternatively, you could use a large metal spoon with a hole drilled through the handle to allow the string to be tied on.

Divide players into two equal teams and arrange them in boy-girl-boy-girl fashion. Hand a key-on-a-string to the first player in each line and signal a start. The first player, assuming it's a man, must pass the key down the front of his shirt, inside the waist band of his trousers and out through one leg. He then passes the key to the woman beside him who threads it under her skirt and then up and out through the neck of her blouse.

Obviously, this description is an oversimplification since it would be a strange party indeed at which men and women were so traditionally attired. Women wearing trousers, or men wearing skirts for that matter, will have to adopt the threading manoeuvre most suitable for their outfit. Either way, the first team to success-fully string itself together in an acceptable manner wins the game.

An obvious and saucy variation to this game would be to insist that players string each other together, allowing plenty of op-portunities for team mates to rummage around inside each other's clothes. Wicked hosts might be tempted to leave the keys in a freezer for a few hours before the game begins. Just bear in mind that any guests who suddenly feel the need to visit the loo after having an ice-cold piece of metal stuffed down their trousers will be significantly hampered by being tied to their team mates.

EXPLAIN AWAY

Object of the game

To explain the significance of a list of people.

What you need

Pens and paper all round.

How to play

A game that involves nothing more strenuous or embarrassing than sitting in a circle and that can be made as racy or innocent as individual players desire – suitable for all.

Each player writes the names of four people on his or her piece of paper; they can be famous personalities, people known to the group or just guests who happen to be present at the time. Players then pass their completed lists to other players of the same sex and the game is ready to begin.

Going around the circle, each guest has to pretend that the list they have was compiled by themselves and that each person on that list has some special significance to them. Taking one name at a time a player is required to explain what role that person plays in their secret fantasies.

For example, a male player who receives a list with the names "Jennifer Lopez, Sandra Bullock, Marge Simpson and Mr Clegg the local plumber" could explain that Jennifer Lopez is the woman he would most like to find naked in his shower one morning, Sandra Bullock is the woman he wishes drove the number thirty-seven bus to work, Marge Simpson would make the ideal mother for his children and Mr Clegg the plumber is the only man he would trust to mess with his ballcocks.

Continue until all players, male and female, have made their confessions and then award a prize to the inventor of the most original explanations.

BLOW ME DOWN

Object of the game

To keep your clothes on.

What you need

A feather.

How to play

Practically any game can be transmuted into a "Strip" version by simply requiring that an item of clothing be removed whenever a mistake is made or a point dropped. This one has the advantage of the increased giggle-factor that comes from requiring players to puff furiously at a feather.

Participants should be asked to sit on the floor more or less upright and be packed as tightly together as possible. The game begins when the host drops a feather in the general vicinity of the players' chests. By puffing with all their might everyone tries to blow the feather across someone else's shoulder, while avoiding the same thing happening to them. Anyone who's breath gives out to the extent that the feather is seen to pass over one of their shoulders is required to remove an item of clothing.

The game becomes particularly interesting when players start to tickle one another when the host isn't looking. The game ends when the host decides or before anyone gets into a real state of undress.

DRINKING GAMES

Drinking games have probably been around as long as drink itself. The Romans certainly played them, as did the ancient Greeks and the even more ancient Egyptians. You can bet that nomadic hunter-gatherers probably played them too after a hard day wrestling with woolly mammoths. The games in this section are supposed to be used to enhance an evening's social drinking not to provide an excuse for excessive alcohol consumption. Please read the following warning, and take it seriously.

WARNING

Next to each game in this section there is a rating that indicates the number of drinks players can expect to take during play. The glasses are there to give an idea of how intensive the drinking is likely to be and range from one to five plus as shown above, they do not indicate a specific number of drinks that players are likely to consume. Actual totals could be considerably more depending on the number of players involved and sheer chance. Any game which has a rating of three or more glasses should not be played with alcoholic drinks.

When the rules refer to "a drink" this should be taken to mean one sip or gulp of drink, not an entire glass full. Before any drinking game, players should work out the amount of alcohol they can safely consume and stick to that limit. When a player reaches his or her limit, they should drop out of the game or substitute non-alcoholic drinks.

Above all, players should NEVER drink and drive. All of these games can be played with non-alcoholic drinks only. It is illegal to consume alcoholic beverages if you are under the age of 18; DON'T DO IT!

BOUNCER

A very simple game of skill spiced with a few wicked rules.

Object of the game

To bounce a five pence piece into a shot glass.

What you need

A table that everyone can sit around, a shot glass or similar small tumbler and a five pence piece.

How to play

Place the shot glass in the centre of the table. If players cannot easily reach the glass in that position, then place it in front of whoever is going first. The player must bounce the five pence piece off the table and into the glass. If he succeeds he assigns a drink to another player and gets another go. If a player succeeds in getting the coin in the glass three times in a row he is allowed to introduce a new rule for the game. Examples might include "The coin must be thrown with the left hand," or "One eye must be closed when the coin is thrown."

A player continues until he misses the glass, at which point play passes to the next player. Any player who forgets a rule when it is his turn automatically gets a drink.

Variations

To make things even more confusing a player who succeeds in getting the coin in the glass three times in a row can choose to cancel an existing rule. Players who forget that a rule has been cancelled have to take a drink.

If the coin bounces off the rim of the glass but doesn't go in, the player may choose to have another go, but if he misses he has to take a drink.

CLEOPATRA

So named because cards are laid out in a pyramid shape, not because it involves poisonous asps.

Object of the game

To bluff other players into taking drinks.

What you need

Two packs of cards.

How to play

Both packs of cards should be shuffled thoroughly before play and jokers removed. The dealer gives four cards to each player from one of the packs of cards. Cards should be dealt face down — players look at their own cards but keep them secret from other players. The dealer begins to lay out an upside down pyramid of cards from the other pack. Pyramid cards are laid out face-up. First one card on its own, then two cards above it, then three, then four and then five in the last row.

With every card that is laid out in the pyramid players check their cards for a match. The definition of a matching card depends on how often you want drink penalties to be given. For the most penalties define a match as any card of the same value, whatever suit. For the least penalties a match should mean an exact match of value and suit. When a player has a match he can assign a drink to any other player. If the match is with the first card of the pyramid he assigns one drink, two drinks if it's a match with a card in the second row, three for the third row and so on up to the fifth and final row.

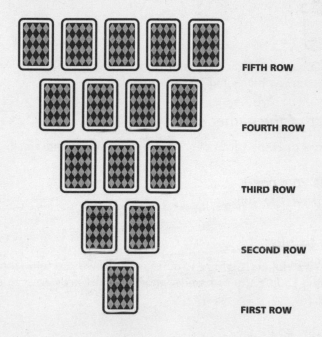

FIFTH ROW

FOURTH ROW

THIRD ROW

SECOND ROW

FIRST ROW

Bluffing is encouraged in this game. A player can claim to have a match for a card even if he hasn't. If nobody challenges the claim, he assigns the relevant number of drinks. If he is challenged the drinking stakes double. When challenged a player must show the card he claims to have. If he has the card, the challenger must drink double the normal drink assignment. If he cannot produce the card, he must drink double the normal drink assignment. Challenged cards must be left face-up on the table, but they still count towards matches with future pyramid cards.

Once the first pyramid has been laid out the dealer lays out a second one. The game ends only when all players have had to show all their cards.

BLACK JACK DANIELS

A game based on Blackjack and traditionally played with American sippin' whisky — hence the name.

Object of the game

To avoid drawing cards over the value of seven-and-a-half.

What you need

A pack of playing cards.

How to play

Remove all jokers, eights and nines and the two red tens from the pack and shuffle the remainder thoroughly. Cards are valued as follows:

Ace: One point
Two to seven: Face value
King, queen, jack: Half a point
Ten: Wild (any value)

The rules are very similar to the rules of Blackjack, except that players attempt to draw to a limit of seven-and-a-half points rather than twenty-one.

Choose a dealer to start – all players must act as dealer in turn. The dealer gives one card to the first player, dealt face-down. The player looks as his card and makes a drink bet for the hand. You can set a maximum drink bet or have a standard bet of one drink per hand. Based on the value of his card the player can ask for another card or stick with what he has. Cards after the first card are dealt face-up. The player keeps requesting cards until he decides to stick or goes over seven-and-a-half points. A player must declare if he goes bust and drink the bet. Failure to declare results in a double drink penalty.

Once the player has stuck the dealer must draw cards for himself. The dealer's cards are always face up. A dealer can stick on one card or keep drawing cards until he is satisfied or goes over seven-and-a-half points. Once the dealer has stuck, the player turns over his card to reveal his total score. The player closest to seven-and-a-half points wins, the loser drinks the bet.

The dealer now turns to the next player and plays again. All cards should be collected and reshuffled before the next hand is played. Once the first dealer has played with all other players, somebody else takes his place.

CHANDELIER

A slightly more complex variation of Bouncer with greater opportunities for making a mess.

Object of the game

To bounce a five pence coin into a nest of glasses.

What you need

A table that everyone can sit around, a large glass (a pint glass is ideal), several shot glasses or similar small tumblers and a five pence piece.

How to play

Place the large glass in the centre of the table and arrange the shot glasses around its base so that their rims touch each other and the large glass. To start with, all the glasses should be empty.

Players take turns attempting to bounce a five pence piece off the table and into one of the glasses. If a player gets the coin into a shot glass he assigns a drink to another player. If the coin goes into the centre glass a shot is poured into it. If a player succeeds in getting the coin into a shot glass three times in a row he can assign the entire contents of the large glass to another player.

SCOUT LEADER

An ideal game for people who like to confuse and humiliate their friends.

Object of the game

To be allowed to go camping.

What you need

One or two people in the group who know the secret of the game.

How to play

One person is the Scout Master – usually the person who initiates the game. There must be one or two other people present who know the secret of the game. Players take it in turns to ask the Scout Master "Can I go camping if I take X" where "X" can be any noun. The Scout Master will only give permission for the player to go camping if he names an object that begins with the same letter as the first letter of his name. For example, Carol asks "Can I go camping if I take a tent" and the Scout Master answers "No, you can't!" If Carol asks "Can I go camping if I take a cooker", the answer will be "Yes, you can."

Example of play

Simon (who knows the game): Can I go camping if I take a sleeping bag?

Scout Master: Yes, you can.

Jane (who doesn't): Can I go camping if I take a sleeping bag?

Scout Master: No, you can't!

Jane: But that's not fair, Simon said sleeping bag!

Scout Master: That's beside the point. You may not go camping with a sleeping bag.

Kate (who also knows the game): Can I go camping if I take a kangaroo?

Scout Master: Yes, you can.

Jane: What's a kangaroo got to do with camping?

Paul (who doesn't know the game, but gets lucky): Can I go camping if I take a pullover?

Scout Master: Yes, you can.

Jane (now thinks you have to name camping gear that hasn't already been mentioned): Can I go camping if I take tent pegs?

Scout Master: No, you can't!

Players who fail to get permission to go camping must take a drink. Players who know the rule, or claim they do, but fail to get permission to go camping must take two drinks. Scout Masters who refuse permission to go camping even though a legal object was named have to take three drinks.

Keep playing until everybody has guessed the rule, or given up in frustration. Obviously players who do guess the rule should be encouraged to keep it to themselves.

REALITY TV

So named because of its similarity to various reality TV programmes.

Object of the game

To avoid being voted out of the game before the last round.

What you need

Cards, dice and a variety of other games for use during "untouchable" rounds. Pencils and a supply of paper for each player.

How to play

Before the first round starts all players take part in another game to decide who is "untouchable" in the first round. You could use one of the games listed in this section, such as The Beer Hunter, or one hand of a card game that everybody knows, or any other contest that results in a single clear winner. The winner of this preliminary round becomes untouchable for the first round of voting in Reality TV.

All players, including the untouchable, now vote for the player they want to be ejected from the game. Players cannot vote for the untouchable. One drink must be taken for every vote received and the player with the most votes is out of the game. In the event of a tie the untouchable has a casting vote. Voting should be done by writing names on pieces of paper and placing them into a container. Once all votes are collected the untouchable reads them out one at a time.

Before the second round of voting another untouchable decider must be played – it should be a different game from the one before the first round. The second round of voting proceeds exactly as the first. The game continues until there are just two players left. There is no untouchable decider before the last round and all players who have previously been voted out of the game vote to decide the winner.

This game is best if it's drawn out to occupy an entire evening. Play long games for the untouchable deciders, this gives plenty of opportunity for people to make their voting decisions and, hopefully, to engage in illegal vote-rigging intrigues.

THE BEER HUNTER

A beer game based on the Russian roulette scene from the movie The Deer Hunter. Extremely messy.

Object of the game

To avoid getting large quantities of beer over yourself.

What you need

Lots of cans of beer.

How to play

Put the same number of cans of beer as players on a table. One can is selected and everybody gives it a thorough shaking. Everybody turns their backs, apart from one player who is elected to sit out the first round. He places the shaken can on the table with all the others and shuffles them around. Once this is done, everybody turns back to the table and selects a can of beer. On a pre-arranged signal every player must open their can of beer. The player who ends up drenched in beer loses that round and becomes the can-shuffler for the next round.

This game can be used to select a dealer or first player for any other game, or it can be played to its bitter end when just one player remains un-soaked.

People have been known to play this game by holding the beer can to their head or under their nose before opening. This is definitely not recommended. The pressure that builds up inside a shaken beer can is considerable and there is a real danger of causing yourself injury if you release it close to your face or ears.

COCKTAIL HEAD

A game notorious for producing the vilest cocktails known to man.

Object of the game

To avoid drinking the noxious cocktail assembled by other players.

What you need

A fairly large glass, a coin and as great a variety of drinks as you can find.

How to play

The rules are almost beautiful in their simplicity. Players take turns flipping the coin. The third player to flip a head gets to put the first ingredient in the cocktail – it can be anything drinkable. The player that flips the sixth head gets to put the second ingredient in the cocktail, and the third ingredient is added by the player that flips the ninth head. The player that flips the twelfth head has to drink the cocktail.

Players adding ingredients should bear in mind that they could end up being the one who has to drink the finished product. Also remember that the vilest combinations usually include non-alcoholic ingredients – vodka with milk and a splash of sherry anyone?

It's not a good idea to drink more than one of these concoctions so victims should be eliminated from the next round.

VERBAL TAG

A version of the world's simplest game, tag, that doesn't involve running around like an idiot and spilling your beer.

Object of the game

To fool other players into thinking they have been tagged.

What you need

Extremely quick wits.

How to play

There are endless variations of this game. Essentially there are three basic legal "moves." Move one tags the person you are looking directly at. Move two tags a player who has just tagged you as long as you are looking directly at them. Move three tags a player who has just tagged you when you aren't looking directly at them. Tags are performed by calling out certain words. In this example tags one to three are performed by the words "Push," "Pull," and "Prop" respectively.

To start a game a player looks directly at another player and calls "Push." The player he was looking at is now "it" and has three choices. He can look directly at another player and call "Push," making that player it. He can look directly at the player that tagged him and call "Pull," tagging the first player back, or he can look directly at another player and call "Prop," also tagging the original player back. Tagging continues until a player makes a mistake (believes he has been tagged when he hasn't) or hesitates too long before tagging. Both earn a drink penalty. After drinking, the guilty player becomes it and must restart with "Push".

Variations

The most common variation to this game is in the words that are used for the tagging manoeuvres. The names of characters from children's television programmes are commonly used, as are "odd" names such as "Luciano," "Bernstein," or "Bonepart." A particularly confusing variation uses phrases such as "To you," "Back to me," and "Back to him" to mean the opposite of their ordinary meanings.

Additional tags can easily be added. If you find the three-move game too easy try adding a fourth tag called "Punt" that tags the person on your right and a fifth called "Pitch" that tags to the left. These rules would, however, require that players sit or stand in fixed positions.

BISHOP BURKE

A game that test powers of concentration and co-ordination to the limit.

Object of the game

To complete a series of repetitive actions in the correct order.

What you need

A table that everybody can sit around.

How to play

The point of the game is for each player in turn to complete the complex ritual toast to the health of Bishop Burke. The toast is as follows:

Raise your glass and say "I drink to the health of Bishop Burke." Replace your glass on the table. Tap the table top once with the forefinger of your right hand, then once with the forefinger of your left hand. Tap the underside of the table once with the forefinger of your right hand, then once with the forefinger of your left hand. Now tap your right leg once with the forefinger of your right hand, then your left leg once with the forefinger of your left land. Lift your glass with the forefinger and thumb of your right hand, take a drink, and replace the glass on the table. Raise your glass again and say "I drink to the health of Bishop Burke." Perform the same actions as before, but tap twice instead of once and take two drinks at the end. Finally, raise your glass for a third time and say "I drink to the health of Bishop Burke." Then repeat all actions, but tap three times instead of twice. At the end, sit down.

Players must complete the toast precisely. Any variation at all from the ritual carries a penalty of one drink and the player has to start again from the beginning. Needless to say, the game gets harder the more rounds you play.

Variations

The ritual toast can be made as complicated or ridiculous as you like, as long as an exact form is agreed upon. Try adding segments that require standing on one leg.

HOBSON'S CHOICE

Extremely simple game-play with plenty of scope for deviousness.

Object of the game

To guess which hand the coin is in.

What you need

Two coins.

How to play

This game is played in pairs. If there are more than two people present, pairs can be formed by circulating around the table – the first player pairs with the player on his left who in turn pairs with the player on his left. With more than two players you need to agree on the number of guesses that should be taken before play is passed on to the next pair – five or six should be plenty.

The first player takes one coin in each hand and put his hands in his pockets or behind his back. He must decide whether to keep both coins (one in each hand), drop the coin in his right hand or drop the coin in his left. He them holds his closed fists out in front of him and his partner must guess what he is holding.

If a player picks a hand that is holding a coin he has to take a drink. If he picks a hand that isn't holding a coin the player with the coins has to drink. The coin-holding player can ensure that the guesser always has to drink by keeping a coin in both hands, but there is a risk. If the guesser correctly guesses that the other player is holding two coins then the coin holder must take two drinks.

BATTLESHIPS

A variation of the classic board game Battleships. Tots of rum all round?

Object of the game

To sink your opponents' battleship using bouncing bombs.

What you need

Eight shot glasses or similar small tumblers, two five pence pieces and a table.

How to play

This game is played in two teams. Teams sit on opposite sides of the table with four glasses arranged in a row in front of each team. All glasses should be filled with drink. The row of glasses is the "battleship." Before play begins one team must be assigned the "head" team, and the other the "tails" team. It doesn't make much difference which team is which except that the heads team goes first.

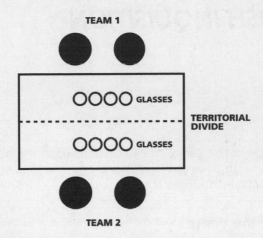

Teams take it in turns to try and bounce their coins into the glasses that make up the opposing team's battleship. Coins must make their first bounce within a team's territory, ie on their half of the table. If a coin lands in a glass an opposing team member must drink the contents of that glass before he can use the coin to retaliate. If a coin lands beyond the enemy's battleship the enemy can use it immediately. When a coin lands short of the enemy's battleship (ie in the space between the two battleships) check to see if it lands heads or tails – the heads or tails team must all take a drink depending on the result.

Once a glass has been drained it must be put back in the line. The first team forced to drain all its glasses loses the game – their battleship is sunk.

Variations

The above rules are fine for two or three players on each team. For more players you might want to add more glasses and more coins.

Drink forfeits can be added for bouncing a coin off the table or for landing a coin in a glass that has already been drained.

SPANISH INQUISITION

Nobody expects this game. Its two chief qualities are humour and humiliation . . . Its *three* chief qualities are humour and humiliation and a fanatical devotion to the bar . . .

Object of the game

To ask questions without answering them.

What you need

No equipment needed.

How to play

Choose a player to start – usually whoever suggests the game. He asks any other player a question, addressing him by name. The question can be as simple or complicated or provoking as you like but it must be answerable by a "yes" or "no." This is an important rule because it restricts the way questions can be phrased, which requires greater thought.

The player to whom the question is addressed must immediately ask another player a different question, he must not answer the question. That player must also think of a different question to ask another player. Keep asking questions until a player can't think of one. The pace should be kept as fast as possible with players only allowed a couple of seconds to come up with a new question.

There is a penalty of one drink for the following infractions:

Unable to think of a question within the time limit.
Forgets to address a player by name or gets a player's name wrong.
Asks a question that cannot be answered "yes" or "no."
Answers a question.
Asks a question that has already been asked.
Asks a question back to the player who just asked him a question.

PLINK PLONK

A very simple and silly game that is almost guaranteed to end with beer all over the carpet.

Object of the game

To toss coins into glasses filled with various alcoholic beverages.

What you need

Several glasses half-filled with various drinks, a supply of coins (five or six per player) and a carpet you don't mind staining.

How to play

Put the half-filled glasses on the floor lined up against the wall. Players stand in a line about five or six feet away from the glasses and take turns attempting to toss coins into them. If a player gets a coin in a glass he assigns that drink to another player, who must drink it immediately.

It's a good idea to vary the contents of the glasses so that some are more tempting targets than others – you can put the stronger drinks in smaller glasses. Also, some of the glasses should contain water or other non-alcoholic drinks but players should not be allowed to examine them beforehand.

KINGS AND QUEENS

A kind of poker with alcohol. Initially simple game play can quickly become fiendishly complicated.

Object of the game

Cards are drawn and rules determine the outcome of each hand.

What you need

A pack of playing cards.

How to play

Remove all cards with face values between two and seven from the pack and then shuffle the remaining cards thoroughly. The dealer gives two cards to each player in turn. The cards should be dealt face down and the player must not look at his cards.

Once everybody has two cards the player to the left of the dealer shows his cards. These rules apply to the combination revealed:

Pair (two cards of the same rank)
The player makes a rule that must be observed by all players from that point on. Forgetting a rule draws a penalty of one drink.

Sequence (two cards with sequential rankings, any suit)
The player assigns a drink to any other player.

Queen and jack (any suit)
The player can assign any number of drinks to another player, but he must also drink the same number.

King and jack (any suit)
The player must draw another card. If he draws a number card he must take a drink, if it's a face card he must take two drinks. If he draws an ace he can pass play to any other player who must draw a card and abide by the same rules.

King and queen (any suit)
All other players must take two drinks,

If a player does not have any of these combinations play passes to the person on his left. Once everybody has turned over their cards and the combination rule has been carried out, the dealership passes to the next person on the left and the cards are dished out for another round.

FOUR KINGS

A drinking game requiring quick wits – inevitably a tricky combination.

Object of the game

To avoid drawing the last king and the hefty drinking penalty that goes with it.

What you need

A pack of playing cards, a table and a large glass.

How to play

Remove all cards with face values between two and eight from the pack and shuffle it thoroughly. Place the large glass in the centre of the table and arrange all the cards face down around it. Decide who is going first and then that player must draw one card from the centre of the table. The value of the card determines what must be done:

Ace
The player to the left must take one drink.

Queen
Play a category round (see below).

Jack
The player to the right must take a drink.

Ten
Play a category round (see below).

Nine
The player who drew the card must take a drink.

King
If this is the first, second or third king to be drawn then the player pours his drink into the large glass in the centre of the table. If this is the fourth and last king then the player must drink the entire contents of the large glass in the centre of the table.

Category rounds
When a queen or a ten is drawn all players must take part in a quick fire category round to determine who has to take a drink. The player who drew the card names a category and one item that fits into that category. Examples might be "Football teams and Arsenal", or "Countries beginning with 'C' and Cuba". Moving to the

left, each player in turn must name another member of the chosen category. The round ends when a player repeats an item already mentioned, names an item that doesn't fit into the category or simply can't think of an answer. He then has to take a drink.

The game ends when the fourth king is drawn and the contents of the large glass are consumed.

CHASE THE ACE

An interesting variation on the dice-rolling class of games.

Object of the game

To avoid getting caught with two dice.

What you need

Two six-sided dice and a table that everyone can sit around.

How to play

Give one die each to two players who are sitting more or less opposite each other. Players roll the dice simultaneously and take the following actions according to the results:

One
Pass the die to the right.
Two
Pass the die to the left.

Three
Roll again.

Four
One drink to the player on the right and roll again.

Five
One drink to the player on the left and roll again.

Six
One drink for the player who rolled the die and roll again.

Because the dice are only passed on when a player rolls a one or a two both dice can end up with one player. When this happens the player must immediately take a two-drink penalty and roll both dice. In addition to the usual results a player with both dice must take a two-drink penalty every time he fails to roll a one or a two on one or other of the dice. Additional penalty drinks should be assigned to any player who rolls a die off the table.

LAND MINES

A drinking game that requires players to remember the position of cards – this could go on for hours.

Object of the game

To make card matches and avoid the "land mine" cards.

What you need

A pack of playing cards with two jokers and a table.

How to play

Remove all the black cards (spades and clubs) from the pack and shuffle the remainder thoroughly. Make sure the two jokers are shuffled in with all the other cards. Lay the cards out face down on the table in four rows of seven cards each (there should be twenty eight cards).

The player to the left of the dealer goes first. He turns over one card and then must turn over another card that matches it. Matches are numerical, so the four of hearts matches the four of diamonds for example. If he gets a match then he assigns a drink to another player and the two matched cards are removed from the table. The player continues turning over cards until he fails to make a match. If there is no match, then both cards are turned face down again and play passes to the next player on the left.

Jokers are wild cards in this game. If the first card a player turns over is a joker then he can match it to any other card. If the second card he turns over is a joker then it makes a match with whatever the first card was. In both cases the player gets to assign a drink to another player. If both cards are jokers then everybody else has to take two drinks.

When jokers are matched and withdrawn from the table this obviously leaves a card that cannot be matched. These cards become "land mines". For example if a player turns over the six of diamonds first, and then turns over a joker, the six of diamonds and the joker are removed from the table. This means that the six of hearts, the six of diamond's matching card, is still on the table somewhere. In this case the six of hearts becomes a land mine. If a player turns over a land mine card as either his first or second card he must take two drinks. Land mine cards should be removed from the table once they have been turned over.

The game ends when all cards have been matched. The second round could be played using some black cards as extra land mines.

THREE-MAN

A game of skill and strategy – both of which should go right out the window after about five minutes of play.

Object of the game

To make favourable rolls of the dice and avoid being the three-man.

What you need

Two six-sided dice.

How to play

The initial three-man must be chosen before play can start. Choose a player by rolling a single die, the player who rolls the lowest number becomes the three-man. Essentially the three-man must take a drink whenever a three is rolled by any player at any point in the game. If anybody rolls a double three, the three-man must take two drinks.

Players take it in turn to roll the two dice. The following rules apply to the results of each roll:

Seven
The player to the left of the roller takes a drink.

Eleven
The player to the right of the roller takes a drink.

Doubles
Two other players must roll one die each and take the number of drinks indicated.

Three
The three-man must take a drink.

The same player remains the three-man until he roles a three during his turn, at which point he gets to nominate a new three-man. If a three-man rolls a double three at any point he can nominate two three-man or make one player a double three-man. A double three-man must take two drinks every time somebody rolls a three (four if it's a double three). If a double three-man rolls a double three, every other player must take a drink and, of course, a new double three-man is nominated.

Any player who rolls a seven, eleven, three or a double gets another go and continues until he rolls something else, at which point the dice pass to the player on his left.

SUNTIRAMAS

Another variation on the dice rolling family of drinking games.

Object of the game

To avoid rolling the lowest score in each round.

What you need

Two six-sided dice, a piece of paper and a pencil.

How to play

Players take it in turns to roll the dice — play is passed to the left. Each player has the option of rolling the dice a maximum of three times. The objective is to get the highest score possible. Simply combine the numbers rolled on both dice to score — rolling a three and a two yields a score of thirty-two. The highest number always comes first so, if a player rolls a one and a two, his score is twenty-one not twelve.

Players must decide whether to stick with their first roll, or to roll again hoping for a better score. The score of the last roll cancels out any previous scores. If a player rolls a second time and gets a lower score, that becomes his score for the round, unless he wishes to test his luck and roll a third and final time.

After everybody has rolled the scores are compared and the player with the lowest score has to take a drink. Additional rules apply whenever the following scores are rolled:

Eleven (double one)
The player is allowed to make up a new rule for the game or to cancel a rule that another player has previously introduced.

Twenty-One (two and one)
The player automatically has to take a drink.

Thirty-One (three and one)
The player assigns a drink to any other player.

THE REDS AND THE BLUES

This one can get confusing, so pay attention.

Object of the game

To dole out drinks depending on the results of competing dice rolls.

What you need

Two easily distinguishable six-sided dice (different colours or sizes for example) and a dozen or so pennies.

How to play

Assign one die as the "drinking" die and the other as the "bank" die. If you can't find two dice of different colours (or different sizes) you could try rolling one with the left hand and one with the right to distinguish them, but that's a lot easier than it sounds and tends to result in spilt drinks.

Each player takes it in turn to roll both dice – play passes to the left. Compare the numbers on both dice to see which die has "won". If the drinking die wins (shows a higher number) the player to the left must take a drink. If the bank die wins, a penny is added to the bank in the centre of the table. It doesn't matter who has the pennies, as long as one gets added to the bank every time the bank die wins.

If a player rolls an evens double (e.g. double four) the player to his right must take a drink based on the sum of the two dice (see below). If a player rolls an odds double (e.g. double three) the player has to take a drink equivalent to the number of pennies in the bank. If they are no pennies in the bank then drinks equal to the sum of the dice are passed out equally amongst all players.

Drink totals

Since this game tends to produce quite large numbers of drinks it's a good idea to come up with a points-to-drinks equivalence table. For example, a score of twelve, or twelve points in the bank, could translate as one whole pint and six points as a half.

ODDS AND EVENS

A quick-fire game that gets everyone into the action.

Object of the game

To avoid calling out the number rolled on a die.

What you need

One six-sided die for each player.

How to play

Choose one player to go first. The chosen player calls out a number from one to six. All players, including the number-caller, then roll their dice simultaneously. Any player who rolls the number that was called must take a drink. The number-caller may choose to call "odd" or "even" instead. On an odd-or-even call players with the appropriate rolls must take a drink, but the number-caller must take two drinks if he rolls an appropriate number. For the next round the next player to the left becomes the new number-caller.

There's a lot of scope for adding rules about dice discipline in this game. Drink penalties could be levied for rolling a die that ends up on the floor, for picking up somebody else's die or for rolling the same number consecutively.

ASSEMBLY LINE

Don't try this one if you don't like the idea of drinking out of somebody else's glass.

Object of the game

To avoid being the last one in the assembly line.

What you need

Three six-sided dice and four or five extra glasses.

How to play

Fill the extra glasses with a variety of drinks and place them in a row in the centre of the table. Players take turns rolling the dice and the following rules apply to the results:

All even numbers
The player to the left of the roller must take a drink.

All odd numbers
The player to the right of the roller must take a drink.

Three of a kind
The roller nominates a player to take two drinks. If he rolled three sixes, however, he must take the two drinks.

Straight (consecutive numbers)
Carry out an "assembly line" (see below).

Players keep rolling until they get a result with no listed rule, then the dice are passed to the next player on the left.

When an assembly line is called for, the player who rolled the straight chooses a glass from one end of the row on the table and takes a sip from it. He then passes the glass to his left and that player also takes a sip. The glass is passed from player to player, with each one taking a sip, until it arrives at the last player in the assembly line (i.e. the player sitting to the right of the player who rolled the straight) who must finish whatever is left in the glass.

BOAT RACE

This one can get unbelievably messy.

Object of the game

Teams attempt to drink more quickly than their opponents.

What you need

Two or more equal teams of players who don't mind getting beer all over their shirts.

How to play

Each team nominates an anchor man before play starts. Teams should ideally sit facing each other along both sides of a long table, but this is not strictly necessary. The anchor man is first in his team's line. Every member of each team is provided with a pint of beer (or some other drink, as long as everyone's drink is the same). The anchor man on each team gets two drinks.

On an agreed signal the two anchor men start on their drinks and attempt to get them down as fast as they possibly can. Once the anchor man has finished his drink he places his glass upside down on the table in front of him and the next team member starts to drink. In one variation of this game players put their empty glasses upside down on top of their heads. Since glasses are rarely actually empty when this happens the results can be amusing. Once the drinking reaches the end of a team's line the anchor man must start on his second drink. The team whose anchor man finishes his second drink first is the winner.

A team may be disqualified if any one of its members: spills an unacceptable percentage of his drink; starts drinking before the man before him has finished; does not completely finish his drink.

WEIGH IT!

One for science-minded drinkers.

Object of the game

To estimate the weight of beer left in your glass.

What you need

An accurate pair of kitchen scales (one with a digital display is best) and identical glasses for each player (pint glasses are ideal).

How to play

Fill each of the pint glasses with the same amount of beer (a full pint is an obvious measure) and announce what each one weighs. Players have a set time in which to drink from their glass until they think there is exactly 16 ounces of beer left in their glass. The glasses are then weighed again and the player who is closest to the target weight wins the round, all other players have to take a drink (from another glass). The weight target is now revised down to 8 ounces and everybody tries again. The game can be continued by reducing the weight target to lower and lower levels or re-started with a fresh pint.

SOAP OPERA

An excellent way to combine mindless drinking with mindless television watching.

Object of the game

To take a drink whenever a certain event occurs in a soap opera.

What you need

A television and a soap opera. It's probably best to record several episodes of a soap opera beforehand (omnibus editions are ideal).

How to play

This can be played "in the background" with another game. The idea is very simple; players must take a drink whenever a pre-agreed event happens on screen. Different classes of event should carry different drink penalties. Here are some examples of drinking rules:

All players take one drink when:

Two characters get into an argument.
Two characters kiss.
A character becomes jealous of another character.
A character lies.
A character has a drink (either alcoholic or non-alcoholic).

All players take two drinks when:

A character goes to a pub or a party.
A character quits his or her job.
A character goes on holiday.
A character attempts to blackmail another character.
A commercial break includes an ad obviously aimed at female viewers (or male viewers if you prefer).

All players take three drinks when:

A character has a near brush with death or is actually killed.
A character gets arrested.
A building catches fire.
A character gets a new boyfriend or girlfriend.
A character is accused of murder or some other serious crime.
A character appears in court.

The game can also be played with movies or with general television. It's a good idea to add a few rules about commercial breaks for extra drinking opportunities.

TOSS-UP

Another simple and quick game that can be played during a dull moment.

Object of the game

To toss a coin so that the result matches the majority of other player's coin tosses.

What you need

A coin for each player (they don't all have to be the same).

How to play

Players toss their coins one at a time. Coins should be left on the table in front of the player that tossed it, showing a head or tail. Once everybody has tossed their coins, tally up the number of heads and tails. If the majority of coins are heads then all players who tossed tails must take a drink – vice-versa if the majority are tails. If all coins come up the same, everybody takes a drink. In the event of a tie, players who tossed tails take a drink. Drink penalties may be imposed for dropping a coin on the floor or for picking up somebody else's coin,

UP RIVER, DOWN RIVER

A simple card-matching game that can carry some pretty hefty drinking penalties.

Object of the game

To avoid matching cards while going "up the river", and to try to match cards going "down the river."

What you need

A pack of playing cards.

How to play

The dealer gives each player four cards face down. Eight cards are then placed face down in the centre of the table in two rows of four. The top row of cards are the "up-river" cards, the bottom row are the "down-river" cards.

The dealer flips over the first up-river card and any player who has a card that matches it (i.e. is the same value) must place it on top and take one drink. If a player has two or more cards that match he must take the corresponding number of drinks. The dealer then flips over the second up-river card. Every card match is now worth two drinks each. Matches for the third up-river card cost three drinks each and for the fourth, four drinks.

Once all the up-river cards have been turned over the dealer flips the last card in the down-river row. If a player has a matching card for a down-river card he gets to assign drinks to other players. Every card matched to the fourth down-river card (the first one to be flipped over) earns the right to assign four drinks. Cards matched to the third down-river card earn a three-drink assignment, two for the second and one for the first. Drinks can be assigned to one player or shared out amongst several players.

Once all up-river and down-river cards have been flipped, the dealer should examine any cards that players are still holding. Anyone caught holding a card that he should have laid down as a match earns a suitably heavy drink penalty.

MATCHBOX FLIP

A fun alternative to dice-tossing games.

Object of the game

To flip a matchbox over a pint glass.

What you need

Full pint glasses for all players, a matchbox, a supply of pennies and a table that everybody can sit around.

How to play

Choose a player to go first. He places his pint glass a hand's width from the edge of the table and balances the matchbox on the edge of the table so that a centimetre or so is protruding out over the edge. Using whatever method seems effective he must try to flip the matchbox over the glass so that it lands on the table. Depending on how the box lands a set number of pennies are added to the bank in the middle of the table. If the matchbox lands (and stands) on one of its smallest sides (usually the ends of the drawer), add three pennies to the bank. If it lands on one of its long sides (usually the striking surfaces), add two pennies to the bank. If the matchbox lands on one of its largest surfaces the player must take the same number of drinks as there are pennies in the bank. When the bank is empty, play is passed to the left.

Drink penalties can be levied for matchboxes that end up on the floor or in somebody's glass.

COORDINATION

A game in which poor coordination results in drinking penalties — not one for the faint hearted.

Object of the game

To remember which hand is yours.

What you need

A table and players with at least two hands.

How to play

Seat all players around the table, or in a long line, and have them place their hands palms-down on the table in front of them. So far so easy. The complication comes in when players have to cross their arms and spread them further apart so that their right hand is roughly in front of the player on their left and their left hand in front of the player on their right.

Beginning at one end of the line, or at any position in the circle, a player performs a simple action with one of his or her hands. This could be as simple as slapping the surface of the table or as brain-bendingly difficult as raising the first and third fingers while keeping the other still. Whatever the action, each player in turn must repeat it using, crucially, the correct hand.

The most common failure here is mixing up left and right and it can be hysterically funny to watch a player gazing with massive concentration at one hand while the other one performs the action. Blunders of this sort, as well as failing to react at all within a reasonable time or mixing up fingers, should be punished with a drink penalty.

BOTTLE PICK-UP

A seemingly simple challenge that invariably results in several players lying flat on their backs wearing bemused expressions.

Object of the game

To lift a bottle using only your mouth.

What you need

Empty beer bottles and a floor.

How to play

Place an empty beer bottle on the floor and challenge anyone to pick it up by grasping the top in their mouth. Sounds simple, until you explain that both feet must remain flat on the floor while no other part of the body can touch it.

Perfectly sober players will find the challenge relatively easy if they adopt a legs-wide-apart crouching stance and use their outstretched arms for balance. Unfortunately, anyone who has consumed more than a modicum of alcohol during the course of the evening is highly likely to pitch forwards at the critical moment and land flat on their face. Failure to lift the bottle results in a drink fine. Failure to get your mouth anywhere in the vicinity of the bottle before collapsing in a heap is punishable by a double drinking fine.

If players are proving too adept at this game try adapting the rules so that the lift must be accomplished with only one foot on the ground and one hand planted permanently on the top of the head. In the interests of hygiene you may want to replace the bottle after each successful attempt, or at least have players use one of their own empties.

SINK THE SUB

A game to be played by the patient and eagle eyed.

Object of the game

To avoid overfilling a floating glass.

What you need

A large bowl or jug and a glass tumbler or pint glass.

How to play

Set up this game of thrills and spills by filling the bowl about three-quarters full of beer. Now place the glass in the bowl and fill it with beer until it just floats. Clearly, this is going to take some experimentation with beer levels and glass types, but the effort is worth it.

Players take it in turns to add some beer to the floating glass without causing it to capsize and sink. Players can add as little or as much as they like, as long as there is a discernable flow into the glass. Any player who commits the cardinal sin of causing the glass to plunge into the depths has to fish it out and drink whatever it contains in as short a time as possible.

Note that nudging the table so that the glass sinks during another player's turn, whether accidentally or otherwise, draws the same penalty as sinking it by overfilling.

IDIOT'S TWENTY QUESTIONS

The trouble with a game like Twenty Questions is that inebriated players have a tendency to forget which famous personality they initially thought of. This version overcomes that difficulty with the cunning application of modern technology in the form of sticky-notes.

Object of the game
To guess the secret identity chosen for you by another player.

What you need
Sticky-notes, pens and a bunch of idiots.

How to play

Provide each player with a pen and a sticky-note and have them secretly write down the name of a famous person, real or fictional, dead or alive (preferably on the non-sticky side of the note). Notes are then transferred to the foreheads of players sitting on the left (or right if you want to fly in the face of tradition). The end result, barring idiotic accidents, is that players can plainly see the identities assigned to other people, but not the one assigned to themselves.

Going around the circle, participants take it in turns to ask questions in an attempt to discover which name has been scrawled on their foreheads. Questions can only be answered "Yes," or "No," as in regular Twenty Questions, the difference is that "No" answers come with a one-drink penalty. Theoretically of course, everybody should only get to ask twenty questions, but it's highly unlikely that anyone will have the presence of mind to keep an accurate count.

Perhaps the most amusing aspect of this game is the way that players who consistently get "No" answers eventually lose touch with reality to such an extent that they beg to be told the correct answer, forgetting that they could simply remove the sticky-note from their head and read it. It's not kind to laugh in such circumstances.

DRINKING CUBED

Not, thankfully, an exercise in mathematics, but a miniaturized version of the game Boat Race that makes clever use of empty ice cube trays.

Object of the game

To empty the compartments of an ice cube tray using a straw.

What you need

A large ice cube tray and several straws.

How to play

In its simplest form this game is a straight drinking race between two players armed with straws. In its most complex form, it's a straight race between more than two players armed with straws – not the most difficult of choices.

Take your ice cube tray and fill each compartment with beer or, if you prefer, a spirit. Most trays have two or three rows of compartments. In a race between just two players you won't be surprised to learn that two rows are topped up with booze. Starting at opposite ends of the tray, each player drinks the contents of one compartment after another through their straws until the entire row has been completely cleared. The first player to reach the end of his or her row wins the privilege of imposing a penalty on the loser.

For a multi-player game use more than one tray and have drinkers arranged into teams operating in relays. Extra fun can be had by adding additional challenges such as requiring players to eat four peanuts off the table without using their hands, or to toss a peanut in the air and catch it in their mouths, before tagging the next team mate in line.

TOC-TOE-TIAC

A game that owes its name to the fact that players are usually unable to pronounce the words Tic-Tac-Toe after playing a couple of rounds.

Object of the game

To make a row of three of a kind.

What you need

Nine glasses of beer and nine beer mats or a large sheet of paper.

How to play

If beer mats are unavailable, make a large Tic-Tac-Toe (noughts and crosses) board on a sheet of paper making sure that each of the nine squares is large enough to accommodate a glass of beer. Otherwise, arrange the beer mats into a nine-square grid to achieve the same effect with slightly more style.

As with regular Tic-Tac-Toe the object of the game is to achieve a horizontal, vertical or diagonal row of three like symbols. Unlike Tic-Tac-Toe the symbols (circles and crosses) are replaced by the following three markers: a full glass of beer, a half-full glass of beer and an empty glass. To further add to the confusion full glasses may be turned into half-full glasses and half-full glasses may be turned into empty glasses at any point.

On each turn a player is faced with the following options:

1 Place a full glass on an empty square (assuming there are any).

2 Drink from a new full glass, turning it into a half-full glass, and then place it on an empty square (assuming there are any).

3 Drink from a full glass already in play in order to turn it into a half-full glass.

4 Drink from a half-full glass already in play in order to turn it into an empty glass.

The tactical complexities of the game can be mind boggling, especially after you've made a few "moves," so it's not a bad idea to play in small teams rather than one-on-one, allowing drinking and mental effort to be spread out among wise heads.

BUNNIES

A drinking game with the built in attraction that it forces players to act like complete fools even before they've had a drink.

Object of the game

To act like a bunny at the appropriate times.

What you need

The ability to make bunny ears with your hands.

How to play

A game with distinct similarities to word-games such as Fuzzy Duck and the distinct dissimilarity that nobody is supposed to utter a word during play. You could insist that players aren't allowed to laugh or smile either, but that's probably asking a bit much.

One player starts the proceedings by adopting a straight face, forming floppy bunny ears either side of his head with his hands and then pointing silently at another player. It's probably best to give some sort of warning before doing this if you don't want people to start staring at you in uncomprehending fear.

Assuming everybody knows what's going on, the pointed-at player is expected to put up his or her own bunny ears and then point at another player. The catch is this: the players immediately to the left and right of the first person to be pointed at must also show a single bunny ear – a right ear if they are on the right and a left if they are on the left. Failure to pay attention or putting up the wrong ear results in a drink penalty.

The worst crime is failing to notice when another player passes the bunny directly on to you and it should be punished with an appropriately severe penalty. To make the game slightly easier players could be required to clap once before pointing at the next bunny-elect. On the other hand, if you are finding this game too complicated you should probably stop now and go home.

THUMB-MASTER

Less of a game and more of a rule of life (kind of).

Object of the game

To watch the thumb-master's thumbs at all times.

What you need

Thumbs.

How to play

When engaged in an evening of drinking games, or any other kind of games for that matter, announce at the start that one guest will act as Thumb-Master for the duration and choose a wily individual to take on the responsibility.

At any point during the evening, no matter what else is going on, the Thumb-Master may place his right thumb on the edge of the table. This may seem like a rather useless privilege until it is explained that the right thumb of the Thumb-Master has special powers. When it is placed on the table in this manner, all other players must duplicate the action with their own right thumbs. The last person to notice and to comply is faced with a stiff drink penalty. Incidentally, a double penalty applies to players who smugly notice the thumb early on but use the wrong thumb in response.

Clearly, the Thumb-Master needs to use his power sparingly and subtly if he hopes to catch anyone out. In some versions of the game, the power of the thumb passes to a new player every time it is used successfully. Variations include the self-explanatory Master of the Crossed Arms, Master of the Itchy Ear and Master of the Picked Nose.

FUZZY DUCK

The granddaddy of all verbal drinking games – largely because people tend to say rude things when playing it.

Object of the game

To avoid slipping up with D's and F's.

What you need

Ears and the ability to speak, or at least mumble.

How to play

No evening of drinking games would be complete without a round or two of Fuzzy Duck, and no round of Fuzzy Duck would be complete without somebody hilariously transposing their F's and D's. Alcohol-fuelled entertainment just doesn't get any better than this.

A player, any player, starts the game by announcing "Fuzzy Duck!" to the assembled crowd. Of course, you could start by explaining the rules first, but where's the fun in that. Assuming that everyone already knows the rules, play continues with the next person on the left. This player has two choices (not including making his excuses and beating a hasty retreat); he can choose to say "Fuzzy Duck!" too, in which case play passes to the next person on the left, or he can say "Does he?" which reverses the direction of play.

When play is reversed, the phrase "Ducky Fuzz" passes the buck on to the next player on the right, "Does he?" reverses it again. Confusion tends to arise when players are thinking "Does he?" but actually trying to say "Ducky Fuzz."

Naturally, using the wrong phrase, speaking out of turn or failing to realise that it's your turn to play all result in a drink penalty. Penalties are very easily incurred in this game, which doesn't help with the overall clarity of players' thinking. At some point somebody will realise that just saying "Does he?" all the time is the safest option — such un-sportsmanlike behaviour should be punished severely.

IBBLE DIBBLE

An immensely enjoyable drinking game that seems incomprehensibly idiotic until you actually try it, at which point it merely seems incomprehensible.

Object of the game

To avoid getting your face covered with burnt cork.

What you need

A cork and a lighter or a box of matches.

How to play

For anyone who doesn't know, when cork is burnt it produced a very fine black ash that was once used by commandos to blacken their faces for night raids, a fact that goes a long way towards explaining the popularity of this game among male drinkers – they get to black-up like commandos while pretending they're doing no such thing.

To play the game the meaning of two phrases has to be understood; "Ibble dibble" means "A player who wants another drink," while "Dibble ibble" means "A black mark on the face." Before play can begin each player should be assigned a number consecutively and one end of the cork should be burned to create a Dibble ibble marker.

Player one begins by announcing, "This is ibble dibble one with no dibble ibbles calling ibble dibble six with no dibble ibbles" – translation: "This is player one (who wants a drink and has no black marks on his face) calling player six (who wants a drink and has no black marks on his face)." Player six then takes up the challenge and issues a call to another player using the same formula.

Undue hesitation at any point results in the guilty player receiving one compulsory dibble ibble (burnt cork mark on the face). His call sign will now include the phrase "with one dibble ibble." Identifying a player by the wrong number, describing him as having more or less dibble ibbles than he actually has or getting your ibbles mixed up with you dibbles all result in a drink penalty. Continue in this fashion until zero hour and then jump into your inflatable dinghies for rendezvous with the sub.

ERIC

A very silly game indeed that requires players to bellow loudly.

Object of the game

To shout more loudly than everyone else.

What you need

A voice.

How to play

Possibly the most imbecilic and socially disruptive activity in this entire collection, Eric is the kind of thing that gives drinking a bad name — well, that and liver disease. Attempting to play this game in a pub or bar is almost guaranteed to result in stern words from the management.

Players should limber-up their vocal cords with a few verses of their favourite drinking song, just to get everyone in the mood for being loud and obnoxious, and then arrange themselves into a loose circle. Player one begins by whispering "Eric" to the player on his left, just loudly enough so that participants sitting nearby can hear. The next player passes on the message in a slightly louder whisper, as does the next, the volume increasing all the time.

Continue until players are bellowing "Eric!" to each other at the top of their lungs. Any player whose shout is judged to be less ear-shattering than the previous shout earns a hefty drinking penalty. At this point the game begins again at a whisper. Obviously judgments in this game are going to be highly subjective, unless you happen to have a device for measuring decibel output.

There's no special reason that you should stick to the word "Eric", choose whatever seems most appropriate to the group – students could experiment with "Existentialism" for example.

TONE DEAF

Combining the joys of music with the joys of drinking.

Object of the game

To replicate notes produced by half-filled beer bottles.

What you need

Bottles of beer (or wine) and musical instruments.

How to play

Players will need musical skills to take part successfully in this game. An ideal interlude for after band practice or when out with a rowdy band of choristers. Musical instruments will also be needed – a piano is ideal but practically any instrument will do as long as participants are sufficiently skilled.

This is one of the few games in this collection where drinking is a necessary part of the set up. Bottles of beer will need to be semi-consumed so that there are several with varying levels of liquid left inside. You could of course play with already empty bottles and fill them with various amounts of water – but where's the fun in that.

The first player selects a bottle and readies his instrument. The bottle is tapped with a spoon, or other metal object, to produce a clear ringing note, which the player has to try and reproduce on his instrument as accurately as possible. Judging the accuracy of a note can be aided by striking the bottle again, but the player is not allowed to change his initial selection.

If a note is judged to be hopelessly inaccurate, the tone-deaf player is condemned to drink whatever is left in the bottle he selected. If, on the other hand, the note is undeniably pitch perfect, then all the other players share out the contents of the bottle.

BUNNY HOPS

Despite its name you'll be pleased to hear that this game doesn't involve leaping about like a rabbit.

Object of the game

To remember where you are.

What you need

Chairs around a table.

How to play

Seat players around the table and give everyone a bit of time to work out how many people are present and to remember it – this may take anywhere between twenty seconds and twenty minutes depending on how many drinking games have already been played.

Nominate a player to start – there's no real advantage to this so it doesn't really matter who it is. The starter nominates another player at the table by referring to him in terms of how many seats away he is. This is achieved by using the phrases, "Hops to the right, four!" or "Hops to the left, three!" with the number representing the distance, so that the first means "The player four seats to my right," and the second means "The player three seats to my left."

In order to avoid titanic arguments at a later stage it is vital that everyone agrees on exactly how seat counting should work. There are two mutually exclusive options; counting the seat that the nominating player is sitting on as "one," or counting the seat next to him as "one." It doesn't make any difference to the game which option you choose, but you must choose one or the other.

Either way, the player sitting in the seat nominated by the first player must recognize that he is next and make his own nomination within a reasonably short period of time. Failure to realize that you have been nominated, thinking you have been nominated when you haven't and, worst of all, re-nominating yourself, all result in drink penalties.

SNAPCLAP-CATEGORY

Actually a lot less confusing than the title implies and great fun to play.

Object of the game

To call out category items keeping to a strict rhythm.

What you need

Players with at least a rudimentary sense of rhythm.

How to play

This looks at lot like one of those thigh slapping, hand-clapping schoolyard games that little girls seem to play incessantly while chanting hypnotic and vaguely surreal rhymes. This is largely because it is, but why should anybody let that stop them having a good time.

In order to play properly the group will have to establish a good steady rhythm of finger snapping and hand clapping. The rhythm should have three parts: finger snaps, followed by thigh slaps, followed by hand claps. Only when everybody has settled into a comfortable and steady rhythm should you attempt to play.

The leader begins with the words "Types of," with the word "Types" coming on the finger-snapping beat and the word "of" coming on the thigh-slapping beat. On the third beat, the hand-clapping beat, he should add the name of a simple category of no more than two syllables, such as "Women" or "Beers."

Once a category has been chosen, players take it in turn to call out a word of two syllables that fits into that category, but only on the finger-snap, thigh-slap beats. For example, if the category called happened to be "Nations" players could chip in with "Al-bania," "Eng-land," "Swe-den," "Hol-land," or "Rus-sia."

Continue until somebody fails to think of anything to add or attempts to pass-off "Bangladesh" as a two-syllable word. Such blatant failings should be swiftly punished with a drink penalty.

BEER CHEQUERS

Not, regrettably, a game in which you are required to check everyone's beer for quality, but a variation of the board game.

Object of the game

To prevent your pieces being taken.

What you need

A chessboard and lots of shot glasses (you can buy plastic ones).

How to play

The idea of this game is to take the gentle, relaxing pastime of chequers, also known as draughts, and turn it into an excuse to drink glass upon glass of beer.

Everybody knows how to play chequers; pieces can only move forward and diagonally (unless they are kings), you can only "take" an opponent's piece if there is an empty square beyond it, multiple pieces can be taken in a turn, pieces become kings when they reach the opposite side of the board (and as such can more backwards or forwards) etcetera. The only difference here is that counters are replaced by shot glasses full of beer, or spirits if the mood takes you.

Remember when setting up your "pieces" that one player plays on the black squares only while the other plays on the white squares only. You will need twelve glasses for each player, four on each of the first three rows. One set of glasses will need to be marked with a marker pen so that they don't get mixed up – this is why it's a good idea to use plastic ones.

Play the game as normal except that when a piece is taken, the player whose piece it is has to drink its contents. When creating kings, the player who allows an opponent's piece to penetrate to the back line of his half of the board has to drink the contents of that piece as well as the contents of another, spare, piece that should be placed inside it to designate it as a king.

SPIN STAKES

Not everyone can spin coins very well; identify these people, pressgang them into a game of Spin Stakes and watch them incur huge drinking penalties – it's something to do.

Object of the game

To spin as many coins as possible.

What you need

Lots of coins of the same type.

How to play

Clear the table of all extraneous rubbish such as ashtrays, beer mats, pools of spilled beer and sleeping people before play begins. Set several coins of the same denomination on the table, ten- or two-pence pieces are probably the best, and issue the Spin-Stakes challenge.

The game is played by two players at a time, a reigning champion and a challenger. In the first instance you will need to elect a reigning champion, preferably someone who is good at spinning coins. The champion states that he can spin, say, three coins on the table top at the same time. This means the third coin must be spinning before the first or second has stopped. The challenger can up the bid to four coins (or more) or can call for a demonstration. If the bid is raised, the champion can up it again or call on the challenger to demonstrate. Continue bidding until either the champion or the challenger will go no higher, at which point the last player to bid attempts to prove that he wasn't bluffing.

If the challenger is successful and manages to spin the number of coins specified in his bid, the champion is penalized with an equal number of drinks and the challenger becomes the new champion. If a challenger fails a demonstration, he has to take the drink penalty. If a champion has the highest bid and succeeds, the challenger takes a double drink penalty, but if a champion fails a demonstration he has to take a double penalty. Continue playing until everyone has at least had a chance to challenge.

PENNY STACK

When they make coins, do they always put the Queen's head on the same side or is it just random? Makes you wonder.

Object of the game

To guess the orientation of pennies in a stack.

What you need

Twelve pennies.

How to play

Just think how difficult life would be if coins looked the same on both sides. So many decisions would have to be reached on the basis of rational thought alone rather than blind chance, what kind of a world would that be? Not only that, it would be impossible to play Penny Stack.

Players take it in turns to be coin shuffler. A shuffler takes the twelve pennies in one hand and jiggles them about vigorously for a few seconds before forming them into a rough stack and plonking them on the table. The player to the left of the shuffler has the task of calling the orientation of each coin in the stack before it is revealed by removing the previous coin. The top coin doesn't count, it's just there to cover the first coin that has to be guessed.

Nobody will be surprised to learn that guessing incorrectly results in a drink penalty. This means that an unlucky player could be facing eleven drink penalties in quick succession while a lucky one could get through the entire stack without getting one – of course this depends on your definition of luck in this context.

Continue around the table until every player has been both a shuffler and a guesser. If you want to liven things up, extra drink penalties can be levied for flinging pennies across the room during shuffles or you can allow players who make three correct guesses in a row to add additional rules.

ON THE EDGE

It might sound simple, but just you try it.

Object of the game

To propel a coin until it is balanced precariously on the edge of the table.

What you need

A fairly large table and a coin for each player.

How to play

The playing surface (table top) needs to be fairly smooth and should be cleared of obstructions before the game can begin. This can be played as a team game or between opposing individuals.

The first players from each team sit opposite each other across the table and ready their coins – ten- or two-pence pieces are generally the best. To ready a coin for play it should be placed flat on the edge of the table so that about a quarter of it over-hangs. By ramming the heel of his hand into the edge of the table a player propels his coin as far as he can across the playing area, but not so far that it shoots off the other side. When his coin comes to a stop a player is allowed two finger-flicks to try and get it as close to the opposite edge as possible, ideally so that it ends up over-hanging. Players must make two finger-flicks after the initial shove.

After one player has performed his shove and two flicks, his opponent attempts to beat him by getting his coin even closer to the opposite edge. If one coin is clearly closer to an edge than the other, the round ends there and the loser draws a drink penalty. If both coins end up overhanging, a decider must be played. Over-hanging coins must be flipped from where they lie and caught in mid-air by their respective players. If this still fails to produce a winner, both players must simultaneously spin their coins on their edges and the spin that lasts the longest wins the game. Move on to the next pair of players and run the contest again until everyone has had a go.

PENNY FOOTBALL

Satisfy your thirst for the beautiful game without leaving the comfort of your home.

Object of the game

To convince your friends that you could have been in the England team if only it hadn't been for your bad knee – and your tendency to sit motionless on bar stools for long periods of time.

What you need

A flat table, some two-pence coins and some pennies.

How to play

Although more reminiscent of a penalty shoot-out than a full ninety-minute kick about this is a game that's guaranteed to have spectators on the edge of their seats and to produce moments that will be talked about for months – well, half an hour at least.

Two opposing players face each other across a hushed tabletop, representatives of opposing teams or simply one-on-one challengers. In front of the player going first there should be a triangle of coins, a penny positioned so that a portion of it is overhanging the edge of the table and a pair of two-pence pieces immediately behind it so that they are touching the penny and each other. At the whistle, the player rams the heel of his hand into the edge of the table so that the penny is propelled across the table and the two-pence pieces are shoved to right and left.

At this point a player should be faced with a table top on which his penny is somewhere in the middle and the two-pence pieces are in forward flanking position. Of course, he could be faced with an entirely different position, but this is the ideal. His opponent must now form a goal by clenching a fist and extending the first and fourth fingers downwards to form the posts. After the initial shove, a player has two chances to finger-flick his coin into the opposing goal. The only problem is that the first shot must pass between the two-pence pieces.

Unsurprisingly, having a goal scored against you incurs a drink penalty. If playing in teams, the losing side may be required to take an additional group drink. Other penalties can be imposed for obvious fouls such as sending coins skidding off the table. Anyone who thinks of an off-side rule should keep it to themselves.

CHEATER!

Perfect for low-down gambler types.

Object of the game

To achieve the highest dice roll, or at least pretend that you have.

What you need

Three six-sided dice and a cup to roll them in.

How to play

The first player takes the dice, swirls them around in the cup and then up-ends it on the table. Taking care not to let anyone else see, he then tips the cup up and looks to see what he has rolled. At this point he is faced with the hard moral choice of truthfully reporting his score or lying like a paddle-boat gambler. Either way, he should keep the dice hidden under the cup. The motivation for lying is that the next player must attempt to beat the dice score, the disincentive is that being found out earns a hefty drink penalty.

Once a player has announced his score, truthfully or otherwise, it falls to the next player in line to choose between attempting to beat the score or challenging by shouting "Cheater!" in a loud and accusatory manner. The options play out like this; if no challenge is made and the next player fails to roll a higher score he earns a penalty, if he beats the roll his predecessor gets the penalty. If a challenge is made that proves to be correct, the cheater gets a double penalty, but if the challenge is unfounded the challenger gets the double.

Rolls are scored by simply totalling up all three dice, so the maximum possible score is eighteen, and the minimum three — players claiming to have scored more than eighteen should be pelted with rotten eggs and forced to drink every last drop of alcohol in the house as punishment for being either complete idiots or blatant liars.

SPOOF

Psychic powers would come in handy here but then, if you had psychic powers, you'd probably be doing something much more interesting than playing games like this.

Object of the game

To guess how many coins players have in their hands.

What you need

Three coins for each player.

How to play

A game that's been around since prehistoric times when cavemen played it using dinosaur teeth instead of coins — probably.

Hand each player three coins or, if you're tight fisted, get them to provide three coins of their own — they don't have to be all the same. All hands are placed under the table and each player must decide whether to place three, two, one or no coins in a closed fist, which is then placed on the tabletop in full view.

One player acts as guesser for the first round and is called upon to predict whether the total number of coins revealed when fists are open (including his own) will be odd or even – for the purposes of this game zero is regarded as an even number. A simple piece of multiplication will reveal the maximum number of coins possible so anyone who guesses a figure greater than this should be made to stand in the corner wearing a pointy hat.

Correct guesses allow the guesser to award one drink penalty to all other players. Incorrect guesses mean that the guesser must take the same number of drinks as there are other players. Of course, if you happen to be playing in a group of fifty you might want to tone this penalty down a tad. Continue until everyone has had a turn as guesser or eliminate players who guess incorrectly and continue until just one stout-hearted but hazy-visioned player remains and wins the game.

THE DICE MAN

A game inspired by the novel in which a complete idiot entrusts every decision in his life to the roll of a die.

Object of the game

To obey the die.

What you need

One six-sided die.

How to play

The idea behind this game is to throw caution to the wind and to entrust your fate to the vagaries of chance. Alternatively you could try sealing yourself in a giant bottle and having it hurled into the sea which amounts to much the same thing but involves less drinking and more suffocating – it's a tough choice.

Before anyone can do anything players must decide on which actions should be taken in the event of rolling a two, three, four, or five on the die. These can be as embarrassing, outrageous or downright absurd as you care to make them. A representative list could look something like this:

Two: Drink a cocktail secretly mixed by other players.
Three: Go into the street and attempt to borrow five pounds off the first person you find.
Four: Go into the street and attempt to give five pounds to the first person you see.
Five: Hitchhike to Burma.

In case you're wondering, a roll of one entitles the die roller to pass the die onto someone else and a roll of six allows the roller to assign a random challenge to another player.

Once the rules are agreed, choose a die roller. This, as all else, should be left up to the die. Every player rolls and the highest scorer wins the privilege – resolve ties by continually rolling until the die makes its intentions clear.

This game qualifies as a drinking game for two reasons. Firstly, and most importantly, a die roller may substitute a large drink whenever he doesn't feel like carrying out the die's instructions. Secondly, players are allowed to change the instructions whenever they feel like it, as long as everyone thinks the replacement is better. As the evening progresses, hitchhiking to Burma begins to look less and less like a bad idea.

BOXHEAD

Brace yourself for hilariously "Who turned the lights out?" jokes.

Object of the game

To avoid having a box placed over your head.

What you need

Two six-sided dice and a box big enough to put over a player's head.

How to play

Another game that relies on the outcome of two rolled dice to decide the fate of players' sobriety and subsequent standing in the community.

Select one player to go first by announcing that the next game involves comparing shoe sizes and then discounting anyone who takes the idea seriously (more conventional methods may be used if you wish). This player sets the game in motion by rolling the dice for the first time. Total the score and act according to the following rules:

Two: Everyone takes a drink.
Three: The player to the left of the roller takes a drink.
Four: The player to the right of the roller takes a drink.
Five: Roll one die; everyone takes the number of drinks indicated by the result unless the result is six, in which case the roller introduces an new rule which comes into effect whenever a six is subsequently rolled.

Six: Nothing happens unless a rule has been introduced (see Five). Pass the dice to the next player.

Seven: Everyone slaps their right hand down on the table, the last one to do so earns a drink penalty.

Eight: Roll one die; the roller must take the number of drinks indicated.

Nine: Pass the dice to the next player.

Ten: Pass the dice to the next player.

Eleven or Twelve: Boxhead! The roller must wear the box on his head until another player rolls an eleven or a twelve and inherits the box.

In some versions of the game the boxheaded player must drink whenever anyone else drinks, although he is not allowed to remove the box in order to do so.

SIXES

One of the few drinking games that requires players to physically move more than a couple of inches, although not much more. Treat it as an aerobics exercise.

Object of the game

To roll sixes.

What you need

Six dice, a table and pen and paper to keep score.

How to play

The game can only be played in teams of two, so you need an even number of players and if there are more than four (i.e. two teams) it should be played as an elimination tournament.

Seat two teams at the table so that team members are facing each other and sitting next to a member of the opposition. A scorer will also need to be present. Each team receives three dice which they take turns to roll. When the game is in full swing this mean that there are six dice clattering backwards and forwards and players need to keep their eyes on the opposing team's dice as well as their own.

The object of the game is to roll sixes and to avoid rolling ones. Every six rolled scores one point and the aim is to amass twenty-one points before the other team. There are, however, complications to do with rolling triple numbers:

Three Ones: Wipeout; team's score is reduced to zero and both team members incur a double drink penalty.
Three Twos: Drink penalty to the opposing team.
Three Threes: Team members must swap seats before continuing.
Three Fours: Drink penalty to the team.
Three Fives: Double drink penalty to the team.
Three Sixes: Chaos; any player can grab the dice and every die grabbed scores a point.

Grabbing triple sixes rolled by the opposing team is of course the most vigorous and exciting aspect of the game. Penalties should be applied when players make a lunge for their opponents' dice when the score is anything less than a triple six.

MIXERS

Works best when everybody is drinking something different – the resulting mixes can be stomach churning.

Object of the game

To avoid the hideous concoctions.

What you need

Six glasses, a six-sided die and players with their own drinks.

How to play

Arrange the six glasses in a row on the table and seat everyone around them. The glasses should all be the same size but it's up to you whether you use large ones or small ones – half pint size or smaller is probably best. Fill the first glass with water and the last glass with beer, or something stronger. Leave the remaining other glasses empty.

Players take it in turns to roll the die. The six glasses represent possible rolls of the die so make sure everyone knows which glass is number one and which is number six. If the glass corresponding to the number rolled is full (initially only one and six) the player who rolled must drink its entire contents. If the selected glass is not full the player must add some of his own drink to it. Players are allowed one roll of the die before passing it on to the next in line. Glasses one and six should be refilled with water and beer respectively whenever they are drained.

As you can imagine, glasses two to five soon begin to fill up with noxious concoctions of beer, wine and spirits. A glass only becomes a potential penalty when it is completely full. It's entirely up to an individual player's tactical judgement how much of their own drink they choose to pour into an indicated glass. Top a glass up to the brim and there's a fairly good chance that somebody is going to be landed with it before the die comes back to you. There's no guarantee of this, but at least you get your own drink back if the worst comes to the worst.

PENALTY DOUBLES

For when nobody can be bothered with complicated rules.

Object of the game

To avoid throwing doubles and sixes.

What you need

Two six-sided dice.

How to play

A good game for getting players into the mood for an evening of drinking games because its penalties aren't particularly harsh and you won't need to be constantly referring to the rules.

Players take it in turn to roll both dice and act according to the scores they achieve. Any roll that adds up to six, such as one and five or four and two, or includes a six, incurs an immediate drink penalty. Double rolls carry their own price. Double twos, double fours and double fives earn drink penalties equal to the number of the double (not the total).

The most feared rolls are double ones, double threes and double sixes. Rolling a double three falls foul of both of the rules above because it adds up to six and because it's a double. Double one allows the roller to assign a penalty of any size to any other player, while double six invites all other players to assign a penalty of any size to the roller.

Continue around the table in this fashion until players feel ready to tackle more challenging games. The usual penalties apply to mishandling dice.

DRINK THE DIFFERENCE

Take the phrases "Roll two dice" and "Drink the difference" and everything becomes clear.

Object of the game

To roll doubles.

What you need

Two six-sided dice and scant regard for sobriety.

How to play

In each round of the game all players roll the dice and take note of their scores, which can be anything from two to twelve. Once everybody has rolled, the player with the lowest score has to take the same number of drinks as the difference between his score and the highest score – in the worst-case scenario, two versus twelve, this will be a whopping ten drinks. It's that simple.

The only trouble with this game, apart from the fact that it encourages rampant alcoholism, is that some players could go for hours without ever incurring a drink penalty – something entirely alien to the spirit of drinking games. The way around this problem is to play the even simpler version of the game in which players roll the dice in turns and are required to drink the difference between the values on the two dice. In this case only doubles can save you from drinking, but at least the penalties tend to be smaller.

MORE OR LESS

As long as you remember that seven is the most likely total to be rolled on two dice you should be okay.

Object of the game

To guess if the next dice roll will be higher or lower.

What you need

Two six-sided dice and a table.

How to play

Before play begins you will need to decide on six suitable forfeits and assign each one a number. Forfeits are decided by rolling a single die so it's a good idea to write them down if you want to avoid arguments later on. The easiest and most obvious system to go for is to equate numbers rolled with the number of penalty drinks that must be taken, but slightly more creative forfeits might be more fun. It is a good idea to get other players to suggest embarrassing forfeits so that when they lose they have to suffer their own evil-minded punishment.

One player is chosen to go first and rolls the dice to set an initial score. Before the next player in line rolls, everyone must call "More" or "Less" depending on whether they think the next roll will net a higher or a lower total. Players calling more should also make a thumbs-up sign and hold it until the roll is made, those going with less should show a thumbs-down. Not only does this add a gladiatorial flavour to the proceedings, it also prevents players from cheating by changing their minds after the roll has been made.

Drink penalties are dished out to players who get their predictions wrong. If the dice come up with exactly the same score as that rolled by the previous player, everybody is due a double penalty drink.

Forfeits come into play only when doubles are rolled. Any player who rolls a double must roll one of the dice again and act in accordance with the pre-agreed forfeit list. All doubles forfeits are in addition to regular penalties.

SEVEN-ELEVEN

Not the well known twenty-four hour shop.

Object of the game

To avoid rolling sevens or elevens.

What you need

Two six-sided dice, an empty glass and a table.

How to play

Place the single empty glass in the centre of the table and have a
supply of beer ready to fill it. This is the forfeit glass; it should be
as big or small as you think you can handle. Choose a player to go
first by whatever method seems most appropriate and hand him
the dice.

Players take it in turns around the table to roll the dice until
somebody rolls a seven, an eleven or a double. Whoever manages
this astounding feat nominates any other player to take the forfeit
glass. The rules concerning the forfeit glass are very strict. No
player may touch it unless they have been properly nominated. A
nominated player must fill the glass before he touches it with his
hands and, once he picks it up, must drink its entire contents
before another seven, eleven or double is rolled. Play must not
continue until the forfeit-paying player actually touches the glass.

If the forfeit glass has been emptied by the time the next seven,
eleven or double is rolled it is assigned to another player. If a
player still has it in his hand unfinished he is punished by having

another half measure added to it. The only way to get rid of the forfeit glass is to drink everything in it before the critical numbers come up again. Fail to do this more than a couple of times and you'll probably be stuck with it for the rest of the night.

CIRCULAR

Take the pure, symbolic beauty of the circle and sully it with booze-related bunkum.

Object of the game

To avoid drawing cards of the same suit.

What you need

A pack of playing cards and a large table.

Arrange the cards face down in a large circle on the table having first removed any jokers. Select a dealer and have him pick any card from the circle at random which he should place face up in front of him. The first player to the dealer's left picks another card and turns it over.

If the new card and the dealer's card are of the same suit, a five of clubs and a nine of clubs for example, then the player that chose it has to take the same number of drinks as the difference between the two cards. For the purposes of this game, all picture cards have a value of ten and aces are valued as one. Cards should be placed face up on a discard pile in the centre of the circle once they have been withdrawn from the circle. The game passes to the next player on the left after each card is drawn. If the drawn card is from a different suit, it is simply placed face up on the discard pile and no penalty is incurred.

The second player to the dealer's left, and every player after him around the circle, faces double jeopardy. To avoid a drink penalty he must pick a card that is a different suit from both the dealer's card and the card picked by the previous player (assuming they were different). If the previous player suffered a penalty, because he drew a card that matched the dealer's suit, the next player faces a double penalty if he draws the same suit again – the difference between his card and the dealer's plus the difference between his card and the previous player's.

Continue around the circle until play reaches the last seat before the dealer. Change dealers for the next round by shifting the role one seat to the right and having the original dealer discard his card. This means that the initial dealer is the first to play under the new regime. Theoretically the game should continue until there are no more cards left, but it's highly unlikely that anyone will still be able to sit upright by that stage.

BEER ANGEL

Surely such things don't exist – do they?

Object of the game

To drink when you are winked at.

What you need

A pack of cards.

How to play

A variation of the blinking game known variously as Killer, Murderer or Assassin, which posits the existence of entities known as Beer Angels — no, you won't find them mentioned in the Old Testament.

Take the same number of cards as there are players ensuring that the selection includes just one ace and one picture card (jack, queen or king). Shuffle the cards thoroughly and deal one, face down, to each player. Players check their cards and then hand them back. The player who receives the picture card becomes the game's equivalent of the Detective and should declare himself immediately. The player who receives the ace is the Beer Angel, a fact that he should keep strictly to himself.

A Beer Angel, in case you've never met one, has the power to force another player to drink just by winking at him. Players must only drink when they think they have been winked at by the Beer Angel. However, since nobody knows who the Beer Angel is, there should be enough cases of mistaken drinking to keep everyone going.

The Detective keeps a close eye on the other players, trying to spot the one doing the winking. The only compensation for this taxing job is that he can take a drink whenever he likes. The Beer Angel would also be wise to take the occasional drink if he doesn't want to give himself away too easily.

Detectives are allowed three attempts to identify the Beer Angel. Failure to do so should result in a suitably embarrassing forfeit, and the same should apply to unmasked Angels. Either way, the game can be played again by simply redealing the cards.

CENTRE SEVENS

If there are fourteen cards in a suit, then the seven is the centre card – kind of.

Object of the game

To lay down consecutive cards.

What you need

A pack of cards and a table.

How to play

Extract all four sevens from the pack of cards and lay them out on the table in a vertical row. Shuffle the rest of the cards thoroughly and deal them out so that every player receives the same number (or near enough).

The idea of the game is to build up complete suits of cards around the sevens laid on the table. Any player who has a six or an eight of any suit should begin but, from then on, play passes in strict rotation to the left. Once the first card is down, the next player must place another as close to it as he can. If he doesn't have a card that fits consecutively he puts down the closest card he can manage, say a four, and is required to bridge the gap by taking the equivalent number of drinks.

For example, player one happens to have a six of clubs so he opens play by placing it next to the seven of clubs on the table. The next player needs to have either a five or an eight of clubs, or a six or an eight of any other suit if he's going to avoid a penalty. If the closest card he has happens to be a three of clubs, he lays it on the clubs line, leaving a gap for intervening cards to be filled in, and incurs a three drink penalty – the difference between his card, a three, and the closest card on the table, a six.

Continue around the table until all four suits have been laid out or until people begin sliding silently off their chairs.

TURN IT OVER

Picture the scene: the fate of the underdog hangs on the turn of a card, will it be fortune or bust – can you stand the tension?

Object of the game

To guess whether the next card will be higher or lower.

What you need

A pack of playing cards.

How to play

It's hard to think of a simpler and less brain-taxing game than this, but at least it involves cards, so anyone watching will think you're up to something terribly clever and grown up.

Remove any jokers from the pack of cards and shuffle thoroughly – the pack that is not the jokers, you can't shuffle two cards. Select a dealer for the first round and allow him to select the first player to take the Turn-It-Over challenge.

The dealer turns over the first card and lays it face up on the table. Whoever is going first is now faced with the awesome challenge of deciding whether the next card will be of higher or lower value – this is also known as blind guess work. Once the call has been made, the dealer flips over the next card in the pack to determine the player's fate. Incorrect guesses earn drink penalties, correct calls avoid them. Players must continue guessing until a card of the same value as the first one turned over by the dealer shows up, at which point the game passes to the next person on the left.

Dealers deal to every player in turn until everyone has had a go. If anyone is still in a fit state to continue, simply change dealers and start all over again. You'll probably find that dealers will have to collect and reshuffle the cards every three or four players.

FORFEITS

Various games in this collection call for players to perform forfeits when they lose or mess up. You are, of course, entirely at liberty to think up your own forfeits, but here are a few ready-made examples that can be used in case of imagination failure. They range from merely embarrassing to potentially psychologically damaging.

- Pretend that you are possessed by an evil spirit.

- Sing a whole verse of whatever song happens to be number one at the moment – including appropriate dance moves.

- Perform a re-enactment of your last trip to the toilet.

- Lick the ceiling.

- Pull a hair out of your body.

- Perform a brief but amusing puppet show using your own socks as characters.

- Have a heated argument with an inanimate object.

- Open the nearest window and bark at passing cars like a deranged hound.

- Give honest personal advice to another player.

- Lick the first white object you spot as if it was the tastiest thing you have ever experienced.

- Caress a random player's buttocks.

- Hit yourself repeatedly with a rolled up newspaper.

- Act as if you have fallen madly in love with another player of the same sex.

- Pretend you are a chimpanzee and attempt to pick lice out of other players' hair.

- Spank yourself and tell everyone what a naughty boy/girl you have been.

- Slither across the room like a snake.

• Perform a brief but moving silent dance piece of your own devising.

• Place an apple in your mouth and pretend to be a roasting pig.

• Dance passionately with a mop.

• Fill a saucer with milk and lap it up like a cat while purring appreciatively.

• Crack an egg on your head.

• Sprinkle salt inside your shirt.

• Impersonate a steak sizzling on a barbecue.

• Sniff other players' armpits and decide who is the smelliest.

• Allow the host to spank you repeatedly and agree loudly when he or she calls you a naughty boy/girl.

• Telephone a close relative and tell them that you have become a monk/nun.

• Collect belly button fluff from other guests.

• Collect a credit card, a condom and a box of matches from other players.

• Sing along raucously to any song selected by the host.

• Walk around the room while balancing a full cup of water on your head.

• Pretend you are a vicious guard dog and vigorously protect your territory.

• Empty your pockets/purse of coinage and give it all away to other players.

• Sing the theme song to a popular television programme.

• Connect every mole on your body using a permanent marker.

• Wear a lampshade as a hat and act like a lunatic.

• Remove all your clothes and then put them on again inside out.

• Get down on all fours and rub yourself against the legs of another player like an affectionate cat.

• Perform a lap dance.

• Greet a complete stranger, or a piece of furniture, as if he or she were a friend you haven't seen in years.

• Stuff your bra or trousers to significantly enlarge your natural bulges.